The New Jersey Adventure

Anthony DeCondo

GIBBS·SMITH
PUBLISHER

SALT LAKE CITY

08 07 06   10 9 8 7

Copyright © 2004 By Gibbs Smith, Publisher

Third Edition

Published by
Gibbs Smith, Publisher
P.O. Box 667
Layton, Utah 84041
1-800-547-9588
www.gibbs-smith.com/textbooks

Managing Editor: Amy M. Wagstaff

Associate Editors: Susan A. Myers, Courtney J. Thomas

Book Design: Robert Holman

American Indian Consultant: Dr. Herbert C. Kraft

Cover photo by Scott Barrow

Printed and bound in China

ISBN 1-58685-364-3

*This book is dedicated to you, the student.
You are the future of not only the wonderful state
of New Jersey, but of the world.
Try to think as far as your heart and
imagination will take you. Learn,
and put to good use, the
valuable lessons of history.*

CONTENTS

MAPS

State Symbols of New Jersey

Flag

The flag has the state seal in its center. It was adopted in 1896.

Seal

Liberty stands on the left of the seal. She carries a liberty cap that represents freedom. On the right is Ceres, the Roman goddess of grain. She holds a horn of plenty representing abundance.

The three plows and the horse's head represent the importance of agriculture. The helmet in the middle represents the state's right to rule itself.

The year 1776 is the year of the American Revolution.

Motto

"Liberty and Prosperity" is the state motto. It is written on both the state seal and the state flag.

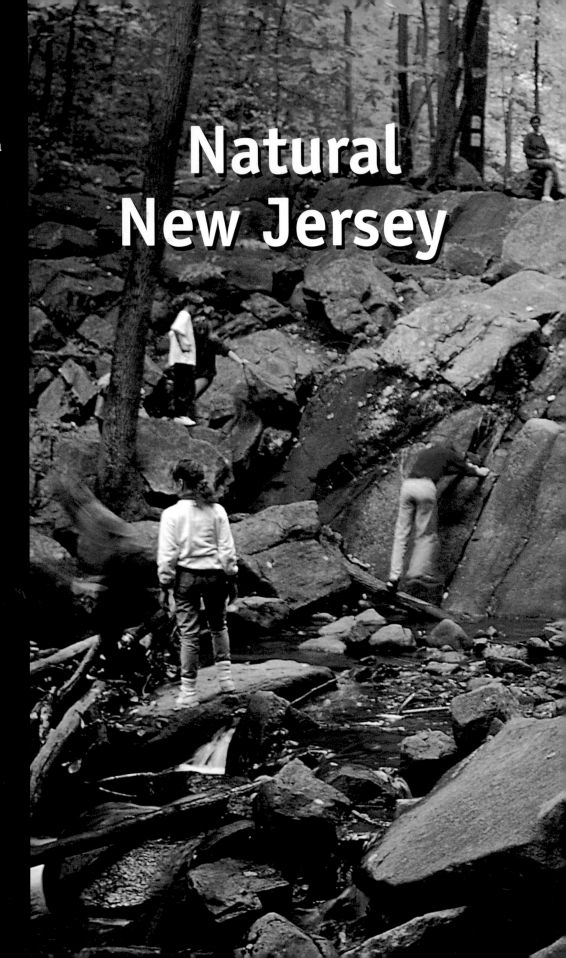

Natural New Jersey

Hacklebarney State Park is a fun place to explore. The land, rock, water, trees, and people are all part of our geography.

(Photo by Walter Choroszewski)

3

The Land We Call Home

NEW JERSEY SEEMS VERY LARGE. Yet it is just one small part of the world. Because we live in New Jersey, it is important to us. It is our home. Millions of people all over the world live in places that are important to them.

In this chapter you will begin to learn about New Jersey by studying its *geography*. Geography is the study of the land, water, plants, animals, and people of a place. First we will study where New Jersey is located in the world. We will learn what the land here is like and how it got that way. We will see how people in New Jersey use and take care of the land.

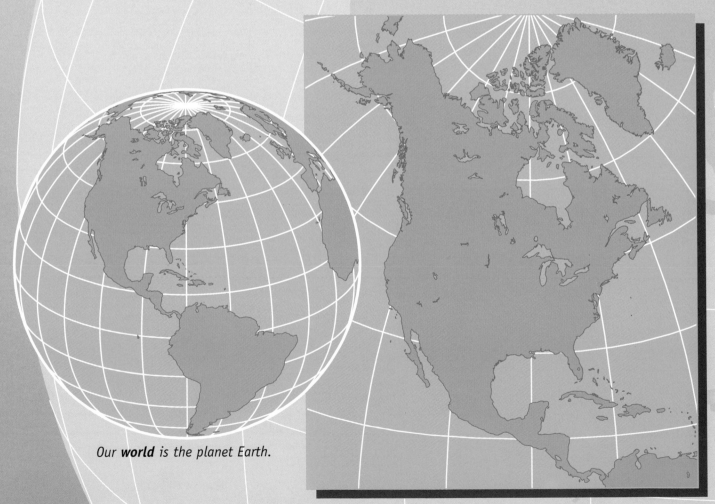

*Our **world** is the planet Earth.*

*Our **continent** is North America.*

Geographers use five basic themes to talk about the ways geography affects us:

LOCATION • MOVEMENT • REGIONS • PLACE • RELATIONSHIPS

Location: Where Are We?

New Jersey is located on one of the world's *continents*. Continents are very large land areas. They have oceans on many sides. New Jersey is on the continent of North America.

New Jersey is part of a *country* on that continent. A country is a land region under the control of one government. Our country is the United States of America. Canada is the country to the north of us. Mexico is the country to the south of us.

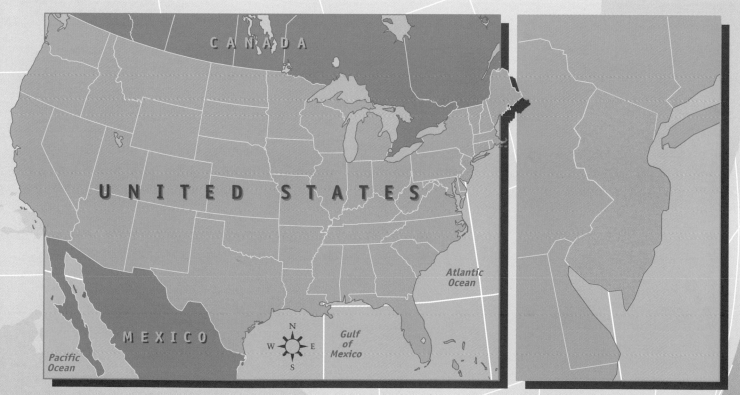

Our **country** is the United States of America.

Our **state** is New Jersey.

Exact and Relative Locations

There are two ways to describe a location:

•**Exact location.** Every place in the world has an exact location that is measured by *latitude* and *longitude* lines. You can see the imaginary lines on a map or a globe. Most of the time, however, we use an address to find an exact location. You might say, "I live at 405 Washington Street, Camden, New Jersey." This tells your friend exactly where to find your house.

•**Relative location.** This tells where something is in relation to other things. For example, New Jersey is **next to** the states of New York and Pennsylvania. New Jersey is **between** Pennsylvania and the Atlantic Ocean. You could also tell someone that you live **near** the Delaware River, or **next to** the school.

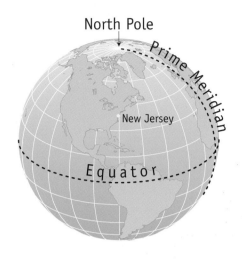

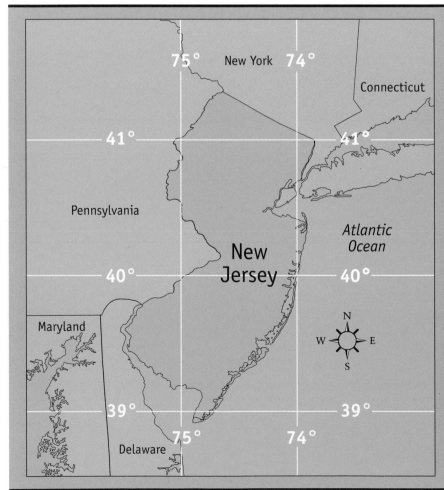

Drawing Lines Around the World

Take a look at a map of New Jersey. Most maps and globes have lines that run up and down and side to side. These are latitude and longitude lines.

- Latitude lines run east and west (side to side).
- Longitude lines run north and south (up and down).

All along the lines you will find numbers. These are the exact latitude and longitude numbers. Each number has a tiny circle by it. This is a symbol for a **degree**. A degree is part of a circle or globe. The equator and the prime meridian are 0 degrees. The numbers get larger as they move away from 0.

New Jersey's main latitude lines are 39° and 41° north latitude. Our main longitude lines are 74° and 75° west longitude. You can trace these lines all the way around the world.

Movement: People, Products, and Information Move

Long ago, Native Americans traveled to far-away places. They traded ideas and tools with other groups. This made them better hunters, fishermen, craftsmen, and farmers.

Today, people from countries all over the world move in and out of New Jersey. Some stay for a short time, to do business or take a vacation. Others come here to live.

Have you ever thought that when people move, they take their ideas with them? When they talk and write, they share information with other people.

In our modern world, the Internet is an example of how ideas and information move. A young girl in Japan can learn about New Jersey while sitting at her computer. A young boy in New Jersey can send information back to her by e-mail.

Does someone in your family make something to sell? Whatever they make has to be moved to a place where someone will buy it and use it. Trucks, trains, ships, and airplanes move things all over the world.

LEGEND	
——	Interstate Highways
——	U.S. Roads
——	Toll Highways

Map labels: 206, Pompton Lakes, Ramsey, Hopatcong, Ridgewood, Paterson, Hackensack, 80, 46, Dover, Clifton, Passaic, 287, Verona, Livingston, Union City, Madison, Newark, Phillipsburg, New Providence, Jersey City, Elizabeth, Bayonne, 22, Rahway, Somerville, Edison, Carteret, 202, Somerset, New Brunswick, Perth Amboy, Hazlet, Keansburg, East Brunswick, Middletown, Princeton, 95, Old Bridge, Red Bank, 1, 9, Long Branch, 95, Freehold, Eatontown, Trenton, Asbury Park, 195, Lakewood, Point Pleasant, Burlington, New Jersey Parkway, Brown Mills, 9, Camden, Cherry Hill, Gloucester City, Lindenwold, 206, Woodbury, 30, Atlantic City Expressway, 295, 322, Glassboro, Hammonton, Pennsville, 40, Vineland, Bridgeton, Millville, Pleasantville, Somers Point, Atlantic City, Ventnor City, Ocean City, 9

N
W E
S

0   25 Miles

Scale of Miles

New Jersey is part of the Middle Atlantic Region of the United States. Do you know why?

Regions: Places with Similar Characteristics

Geographers divide large areas of the world into smaller parts. We call these parts regions. Regions are places that have certain things in common, or that are alike in some way.

A region can be as large as a continent or as small as your neighborhood. The United States of America is a region. It is divided up into smaller regions. New Jersey is a region. Your

The Four Land Regions in New Jersey

Part of the great Appalachian Trail goes across the Kittatinny Mountains.

Evening sun shines on Jenny Jump State Forest. Notice the rolling hills with farmland in the distance.

▲ Photos by Tom Till

Appalachian Ridge and Valley

The Kittatinny Mountains are part of the great Appalachian Ridge. The Delaware River flows through the Delaware Water Gap and cuts into the ridge. High Point on Kittatinny Mountain is the highest place in the state. You can stand on the mountain and see into New York. This is the state's most rugged land. It is wild and beautiful. It is covered with forests. In the valleys next to the mountains are the dairy lands where cows graze on the rich grasses.

New Jersey Highlands

The highlands are a series of flat-topped rock ridges. The ridges are separated from each other by narrow valleys. Rivers flow through the green valleys. Most of New Jersey's lakes are in the Highlands Region. People have built homes around the lakes. Other people by the thousands have come to live in the peaceful mountain valleys.

town is a region. There are also desert regions and mountain regions. There are coastal regions. You can live in many regions at the same time.

Land Regions

If you were a bird flying over the state, you would see that there are four very different kinds of land. That's a lot for such a small state! We call these land regions. Each land region has mostly one type of landform, though it can have others.

Trenton is New Jersey's capital city.

Sand ripples make interesting patterns after a storm at Island Beach State Park.

Piedmont Plain

At the edge of the mountains, rivers tumble down onto low hills and a flat plain. The rivers spread across the flat valleys to provide water for cities and farms. Most of New Jersey's major cities are in this region. Trenton, the state capital, is here. Newark, the state's largest city, is also built on the plain. Most of the major colleges and universities are near the cities. So are most of the state's industries. Many famous events in history took place here. It is an exciting place, with much to see and do.

Atlantic Coastal Plain

This land is a huge flat region that can be divided into two parts. The inner coastal plain has rich fertile soil. It gave New Jersey its reputation as a garden state. Many farms and orchards and dairy cattle are part of this region.

The outer coastal plain does not have much good soil. It has mostly sand. Most plants don't grow well there. The plain has many small hills, then levels off out to the ocean. Here is the famous Jersey Shore. Near the ocean are shallow salt marshes. Out in the ocean are islands. People live on many of the islands.

Part of the Coastal Plain is called the Pine Barrens. It is a wild place of forests and swamps. Not many people live there.

What do you think?

Why do you think people usually build homes and cities on flatter land near water? Consider industry, transportation of goods and people, and personal needs.

"One spring day I visited . . . the Pine Barrens. I climbed a fire tower. The world was green, a lawn of cypress and pine. . . . The land is our teacher. It instructs us in the value of things that can't be bought or sold."
—Bill Bradley, former U.S. Senator from New Jersey

People enjoy canoeing on the Oswego River in the Pine Barrens.

Place: What Is New Jersey Like?

All places are like other places in some ways. All places are different in some ways. All places have a *natural environment*. The natural environment includes such things as land, rocks, trees, rivers, oceans, beaches, and even plants and animals.

New Jersey is a place of mountains in the north and flat land in the south. You and your family can get into a car and see both types of land in one day. Many kinds of plants and animals live on the different kinds of land.

Places also have *human features*. People build strong bridges over rivers. They plant orchards of peach trees. The human features include crowded cities and lonely lighthouses.

New Jersey's Land

Land:	7,505 square miles
Water:	700 square miles
Greatest length:	166 miles
Narrowest width:	32 miles
Widest width:	75 miles

"You can drive from end to end in less than three hours. The Garden State offers great rewards to those who look for them."

—Thomas M. O'Neill

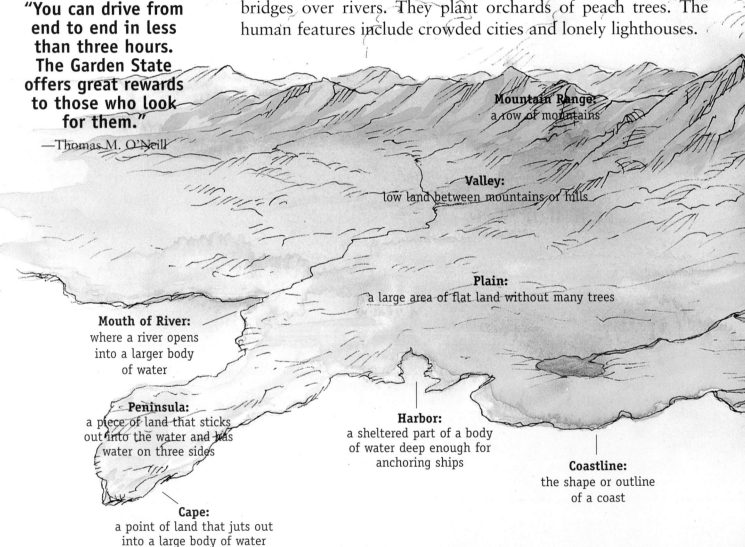

Mountain Range:
a row of mountains

Valley:
low land between mountains or hills

Plain:
a large area of flat land without many trees

Mouth of River:
where a river opens into a larger body of water

Peninsula:
a piece of land that sticks out into the water and has water on three sides

Cape:
a point of land that juts out into a large body of water

Harbor:
a sheltered part of a body of water deep enough for anchoring ships

Coastline:
the shape or outline of a coast

Almost Surrounded by Water

When early explorers came here, they thought that New Jersey was an island. Islands have water all around them. New Jersey is really a *peninsula*. Do you know what that means? A peninsula is a finger of land that has water on three sides. Today, you don't have to drive too far to see either the Atlantic Ocean, Hudson River, Delaware River, or Delaware Bay. It is easy to see why the explorers thought they had found an island.

There is also a lot of water inside our state. There are about 800 lakes and ponds. There are about 100 rivers and creeks.

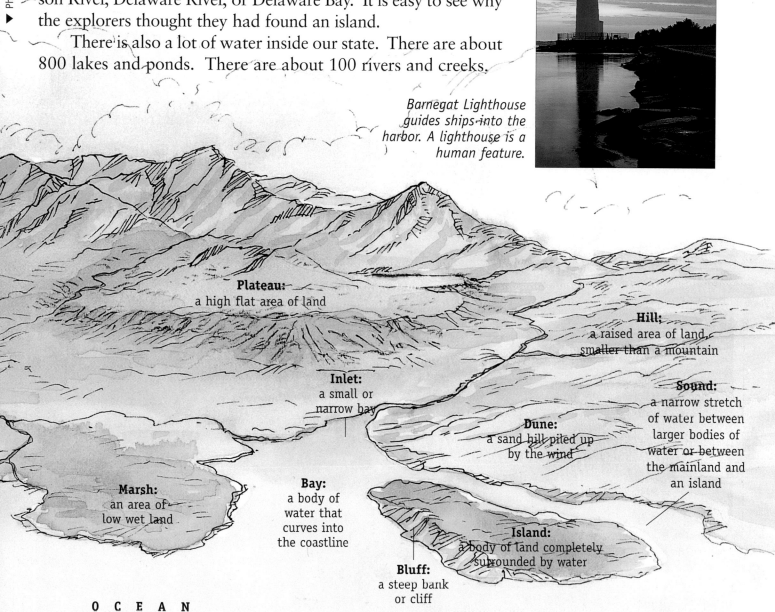

Photo by Tom Till

Barnegat Lighthouse guides ships into the harbor. A lighthouse is a human feature.

Plateau: a high flat area of land

Hill: a raised area of land, smaller than a mountain

Inlet: a small or narrow bay

Sound: a narrow stretch of water between larger bodies of water or between the mainland and an island

Dune: a sand hill piled up by the wind

Marsh: an area of low wet land

Bay: a body of water that curves into the coastline

Island: a body of land completely surrounded by water

Bluff: a steep bank or cliff

OCEAN

Because the land is so low and so near the ocean and rivers, there are many marshes or wetlands. People can't live in the wet muddy marshes, but some birds and other animals find it a wonderful place to live.

Look at the map and study the water around New Jersey. What rivers are our borders? What bay is one of our borders? What ocean is one of our borders? Where is New Jersey joined to the rest of the land? What are the longest rivers? Which rivers are closest to your home?

Water adds interest and beauty to the land. Rivers and oceans are also very important for transportation. We use our water systems to ship goods to and from cities and countries around the world.

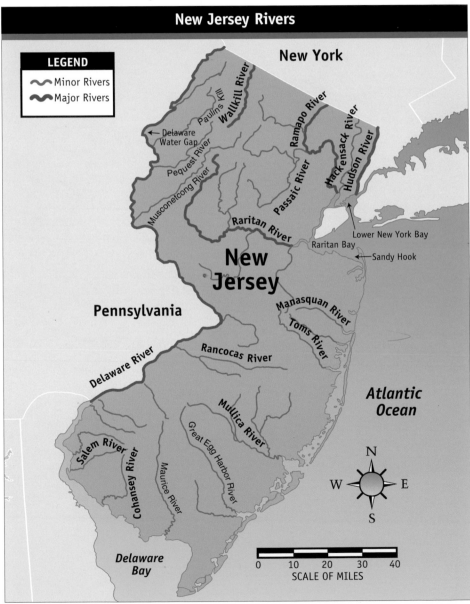

New Jersey Rivers

LEGEND
~ Minor Rivers
~ Major Rivers

New York

Wallkill River
Paulins Kill
Ramapo River
Hackensack River
Hudson River
Delaware Water Gap
Pequest River
Passaic River
Musconetcong River
Raritan River
Lower New York Bay
Raritan Bay
Sandy Hook

New Jersey

Pennsylvania

Manasquan River
Toms River
Rancocas River

Delaware River

Atlantic Ocean

Mullica River

Salem River
Cohansey River
Maurice River
Great Egg Harbor River

N
W   E
S

Delaware Bay

SCALE OF MILES
0   10   20   30   40

Photo by Tom Till

Great Falls on the Passaic River is the second largest waterfall in all of North America. In 1680, an Indian guide showed the falls to two Dutch missionaries. One of the missionaries wrote in a journal:

"We heard the noise of water; and [climbing] up to the top we saw the falls below us, a sight to be seen in order to observe the power and wonder of God."

Great Falls •

Great Falls is on the Passaic River.

Natural New Jersey

The Magnificent Atlantic

Have you ever splashed in the ocean waves?

Did you wonder who lived on the other side of the ocean?

As you picked up shells and smelled the seaweed, did you think about the fish that live in the cold rolling water? Did you taste the water?

Did you smell the ocean air? What did you hear? What did you feel?

Plenty of Water

Ocean waves are exciting to ride on and fun to run from in bare feet. But waves are powerful. They cut away shorelines, carrying away sand and rock. Waves make sea cliffs and sea caves. Sometimes they dump sand in another place, making sand bars. Because of ocean waves, the shore is constantly changing.

Oceans never dry up because when water *evaporates*, it falls back into the ocean as rain. Or, the evaporated water is carried by winds across the land. There it falls as rain or snow, melts into the ground, runs into rivers, and finally finds its way back to the ocean.

School children enjoy the beach and the surf at Belmar.

▲ Photo by Scott Barrow. Background photo of Sandy Hook by Tom Till

Ships carrying goods across the ocean stop at Cold Spring Harbor, Cape May.

Photo by Walter Choroszewski

A Home for Fish

The ocean is an important source of food. Even families far away from oceans eat frozen fish, canned fish, and fresh fish. What do the fish eat? Larger fish eat smaller fish. Fish also eat plants.

Not all the animals in the sea are fish. Animals that have shells, such as clams, shrimp, and lobsters, are not true fish. They are shellfish. They have hard shells instead of bones. True fish have bones and scales. Gills allow them to breathe under water. Whales and dolphins are not fish at all. They are mammals. They do not have scales. Since they don't have gills, they come up out of the water to breathe air.

Photo by Scott Barrow

Have you ever seen anyone belly boarding on ocean waves?

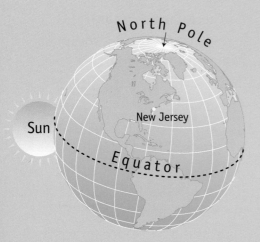

North Pole

Sun

New Jersey

Equator

Our Climate

Climate is very important to a place. Climate is what the weather of a place is like over a long period of time. The *average* amount of rain or snow that falls in your yard is part of the climate. The average temperatures in summer and winter when you want to play outside are part of climate. Even the wind blowing from the ocean affects the climate.

There are many things that affect climate:

• **Distance from the equator.** The equator is an imaginary line that goes around the center of the earth. This is where the earth is the "fattest" and closest to the sun. It is very hot on the equator. New Jersey is not close to the equator, so it is not warm all year long. It is not close to either the North or South Pole, where there is ice all year long. New Jersey is about halfway between the equator and the North Pole.

• **Elevation.** *Elevation* means how high the land is above the level of the ocean. We call the level of the ocean *sea level*. This is the starting point for measuring elevation. Most of New Jersey has a low elevation.

• **Large lakes and the ocean.** Land near a large body of water usually gets more *precipitation* (rain and snow) than other places. The air also holds more water there, even when it is sunny. If you hear someone say, "It is so hot and *humid* today" it means there is a lot of moisture in the air.

Where does the water come from? Water in Delaware Bay and the Atlantic Ocean is always evaporating. It goes into the air and is carried by wind across the land.

Water affects our climate in another way. Water changes temperature more slowly than air does. It stays warmer longer, and it helps keeps the land near it warmer, too. This is why places near oceans usually have milder climates than places in the center of the United States. Aren't you glad that New Jersey is near an ocean?

Weather is the rain, snow, or sunshine at one time. Climate is the weather over a long time.

"This is the fourth day of a dark . . . storm, wind and rain. . . . The dark smoke-colored clouds roll in furious silence . . . the wind steadily keeps up its hoarse, soothing music over my head—Nature's mighty whisper."

—Walt Whitman, *Specimen Days*

Because New Jersey is near the ocean, we have weather that some other places don't. We often have heavy snows. The snow is fun to play in, but your parents don't like to drive when it snows. It's dangerous! Sometimes the moisture in the air freezes right on homes and trees and wires. This is also dangerous.

Have you ever heard the howl of a hurricane? It can be very scary! The wind screams. Rain rushes down. The ocean waves ride high and furious. Luckily, hurricanes don't happen often.

Highs and Lows

Highest: High Point Kittatinny Mountains 1,803 ft.

Lowest: Atlantic Coast, sea level

Coldest temperature: -34° at River Vale (1904)

Hottest temperature: 110° at Runyon (1936)

▶ Photo by Tom Till

From High Point you can see New York, New Jersey, and Pennsylvania. High Point is New Jersey's highest elevation.

New Jersey's Plants

If you were to divide New Jersey into five equal pieces, two of the pieces would be covered with forests. The other three pieces would also have trees, but mostly bushes and grasses.

What kinds of plants grow naturally in New Jersey? The next time you travel away from a city, look at the trees, bushes, grasses, weeds, and wildflowers that grow there. As you explore beaches and riverbeds, see what large and small plants live there. When you go to the mountains, see what different plants grow there. Notice how they change during different seasons of the year.

What do you think?

Plants that grow high on the mountains are different from plants that grow on the low land near the coast. Do you know why different plants grow in different places? Think about the elevation, the temperature, the amount of moisture in the air, and the kinds of soil or sand in each place.

▲ Photo by Walter Choroszewski

Harvesting cranberries in shallow water is big business in the Garden State.

The Garden State

New Jersey has a nickname. It is called "the Garden State." There are about 9,000 farms in the state. Many of them are small family farms. Our climate is important for everyone, but it is really important for farmers. Plants need a lot of sunshine. Most of New Jersey has many months of warm growing weather. Most years have plenty of rain for crops. We have fertile soil and flat land. This makes growing crops easier.

What is your favorite vegetable? When was the last time you ate asparagus, bell peppers, spinach, lettuce, cucumbers, corn, or tomatoes? They are all grown in New Jersey. Fruits also grow well in our state. Do you like blueberry pie with ice cream? Do you drink cranberry juice? Do you like juicy apples? Our state is famous for its delicious peaches.

What happens to the fruits and vegetables after the farmers harvest them? Many are sold fresh to stores and restaurants. Most of them are frozen or canned before they are shipped to stores. New Jersey helps feed the world.

Farm crops such as hay, corn, soybeans, and wheat are also grown in New Jersey. They are important for feeding animals and people.

Along with vegetables and fruits, our farmers raise dairy cows and produce milk. There are also poultry farms in some places. Do you like scrambled eggs for breakfast? The last one you ate might have been from a farm in your own state.

Corn is an important farm crop.

Photo by John Lynn

Have you ever seen a prickly porcupine?

A red fox likes to hide from people.

A raccoon washes its food in a muddy stream.

Deer live in the mountains and hills.

▲ Raccoon and porcupine photos by Lynn Chamberlain

New Jersey's State Symbols

Insect: honeybee

Bird: eastern goldfinch

Animal: horse

New Jersey's Animals

What animals do you have for pets? Black bears and coyotes? Skunks and raccoons? Of course not! They are wild animals. Many of them live in New Jersey. White-tailed deer live here. Smaller animals such as squirrels, chipmunks, foxes, opossums, and cottontail rabbits share *habitats*. A habitat is the natural home of an animal.

A long time ago, Native Americans caught fish to eat. People do the same thing today. Now, however, we usually don't catch the fish ourselves. Other people go out in fishing boats and catch fish for a living. Then we buy the fish at the store.

Very large animals also live in the deep ocean water. You

are lucky if you have ever seen a whale out in the ocean. Each spring, dolphins give birth to their babies in Delaware Bay.

Some animals like to live on the land in wet habitats. Do you know what a *reptile* is? A reptile moves on its belly (snakes) or crawls on very short legs (turtles and crocodiles). It has scales or a bony plate covering its body.

Have you ever caught a frog at the nearest pond? Frogs and toads are *amphibians.* They also live in the marshes and near the rivers. Their babies live and breathe in the water, but the adults must breathe air.

Are you a bird watcher? There are many kinds of birds to see in our state. You probably already know that when cold weather is coming many birds go south to warm climates. They return in the spring. The Atlantic Flyway is a path that birds take when they fly north and south. New Jersey is right on the flyway.

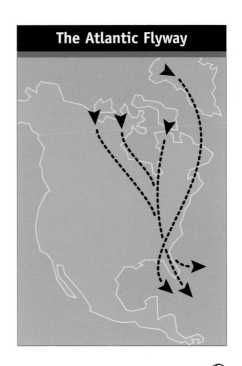

The Atlantic Flyway

Many animals and birds live in New Jersey's wet places.

Ancient Times

Long ago our land was quite different from what it is now. *Geologists* are scientists who study layers of rock to learn more about the past. They learn how forces inside the earth have changed the land. They study how water and wind and temperature have made changes.

When geologists find seashells in a layer of rock, they know that large seas once covered that land. At one time the Appalachian Mountains were under ocean water. In fact, scientists think that all of New Jersey was under water more than once.

Large animals once lived in the ocean. These animals are all extinct now.

Age of Dinosaurs

When the land and the climate were very different from what they are now, different plants and animals lived here. At one time, huge dinosaurs roamed over the land. The dinosaurs were reptiles. Some of them ate plants and some ate other animals. At least four kinds of land-loving dinosaurs lived in New Jersey.

There were other beasts, too. Giant crocodiles lived in the swamps. Other large animals lived in the ocean. They looked like monsters. One geologist described the animals this way:

> *Waters were dominated by huge reptiles. . . .*
> *Elasmoraurs, 50 feet long, . . . with short flippers and*
> *long flat tail. . . . Besides the sea reptiles there were*
> *sharks, whose teeth . . . measure 4 to 5 inches long and*
> *3 inches wide.*
>
> —Dr. Henry B. Kummel

America's First Dino Skeleton

The first complete dinosaur skeleton ever found in America was dug up on a farm near Haddonfield in 1858. Scientists called it Hadrosaurus. It was about 28 feet high and 30 feet long. Measure this on your school playground to see how large the Hadrosaurus was. The bones were taken by wagon to a museum in Philadelphia. There is a model of Hadrosaurus in the State Museum at Trenton.

What Did They Eat?

Today, some wild animals eat plants and others eat meat. Their meat is other animals they kill. It was the same during the time of the dinosaurs.

Carnivores eat meat.
Herbivores eat plants.

Marl pits are places where there is a lot of loose sand and clay. Ancient animals got stuck in the pits. Many of their bones have been found there.

• Haddonfield

A Mighty Glacier

Long before any people lived where you live now, a thick sheet of ice called a *glacier* formed in the icy polar regions of the earth. As the air got colder and colder, the ice got thicker and grew larger. Its heavy weight caused it to move slowly over the land. It covered up the soil and the plants.

Tall mountains slowed down the moving glacier. The ice moved faster through the valleys. Everywhere the glacier went it carried rocks and earth. The shoreline was much farther out to sea than it is now. This was because so much water was frozen in the glaciers.

That time in history is called the Ice Age. Over and over again the glaciers melted and then came back. At least twice the glaciers came as far as the place we now call New Jersey.

▲ Photo by Tom Till

Tripod Rock is a large boulder balanced on three smaller rocks. It was left behind by a glacier.

What happened when the temperature of the air got warmer and the glaciers started melting? Thick layers of rock, sand, and clay were left behind. This formed rocky ridges and hills. Sometimes the ridges of rocks and earth made a natural dam which stopped rivers from flowing. New lakes were formed. As the lakes filled with more and more water, they overflowed the dams and made new paths to the ocean. New rivers were formed. In some places the water just spread out over the land. The land became a wet and swampy marsh.

Volcanoes used to be part of our ancient landscape.

Matilda the Mastodon

At the end of the Ice Age, very large animals lived on the land and in the ocean. On the land, huge mastodons lived in herds. They were hunted by some of the first people to come here. About 150 years ago, in 1850, six mastodon skeletons were found on a farm. Others were found later in other places.

A skeleton of "Matilda" was found in Vernon while men were draining a pond. Scientists think that Matilda followed a melting glacier north. She sank into the wet swampy land around the glacier and quickly died.

After many years the weather got even warmer. For reasons no one knows, the mastodons disappeared forever.

Mastodons and mammoths used to roam the land.

The first mastodon skeletons in New Jersey were dug up on a farm near Hackettstown. Others were found later at Mannington. The bones were moved to Rutgers University.

• Hackettstown

Rutgers University

• Mannington

Relationships: People Use and Change the Land

Geographers study the relationship between the land and people, plants, and animals over time. Our land is always changing. Some change is very slow. *Erosion* and wind slowly wear away rock and soil. Natural events such as hurricanes and floods happen fast. Sometimes when there is a lot of rain the rivers and streams flood out over the land.

People also change the land. They cut down trees. They build cities and highways. They plant new trees. They build bridges and dams and make reservoirs. They dig into the ground to get coal and iron. These things can be important for people. They provide things we all need, including homes and jobs.

If people and industries are not careful, though, they can harm the environment. There was a time when people did not take care of the land. They thought people could never use up all the grass, trees, and other resources. They thought there would always be plenty of fresh air and clean water. They

"In one of the world's most populated regions, New Jersey's wild and natural areas take on great value. Our remaining natural lands stand like endangered species."

—Tom Till, photographer

▲ Photo by Scott Barrow

Burning garbage pollutes the air if it is not done properly. Is this a place you would want to visit?

didn't think it would matter if they left trash on city streets and on the sandy beaches. Their cars and factories polluted the air. They allowed industries to dump waste into rivers and the ocean.

Eventually, people began to understand how important it is to use natural resources wisely. They passed new laws to make it illegal for people or factories to pollute the air and water. They set aside some land for state parks and wildlife refuges. Today, most people are working together to keep our state a good place to live.

It is up to everyone to help *conserve* natural resources and protect the environment. Even you can help. You can stop littering. You can recycle cans and paper. You can turn off lights and televisions when you aren't using them. Everyone can help prevent forest fires caused by humans. Everyone can be careful to take care of New Jersey.

Photo by Scott Barrow

Clean air and water are important natural resources.

About twenty percent of the state's land is protected wilderness. This means that the land, water, plants, and animals live there in a natural way. People can visit the land, but it is against the law to change it in any way.

Maps show the locations of places. There are many wonderful places in New Jersey. Do you live in one of these cities? Which cities are closest to you? Which cities are the farthest away from you? Are there any rivers near you? How many miles are you from the ocean?

The New Jersey Adventure

Reading a Map

There are many kinds of maps. Can you think of some? Perhaps you first thought of a road map. You might use it on a vacation trip. Your class has maps of the world and the United States. Maps help us get where we want to go. They help us understand where places are.

It is important to know how to read a map. Most maps have *symbols* you need to know about. Here are some of them:

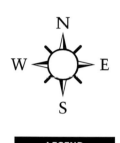

LEGEND
★ State Capital
● Major City
〜 River

0   10   20   30   40
SCALE OF MILES

• **Compass:** Maps show the directions north, south, east, and west. You'll find these directions on a compass symbol. Most maps have north at the top. It is easier to read a map if you put the map so that you and the map are facing north. Then west will be on your left and east will be on your right. Where will south be?

• **Legend or Key:** Mapmakers use symbols to stand for certain things such as cities, rivers, freeways, campgrounds, and airports. Whenever there are symbols, there is a key or legend that explains what the symbols mean. What do the symbols on this legend represent? Find the symbols on the map.

• **Scale of Miles:** To show us distances, or how far apart places really are, mapmakers use a scale of miles. One inch on a map might mean 100 miles on the real land. Or one inch might stand for 1,000 miles, or even more. Look at this map and see how many miles are equal to one inch. Look at a globe and see how many miles one inch stands for.

Chapter 1 Review

1. Give the exact and relative location of your home.

2. How many different land regions does New Jersey have? Which one do you live in?

3. What is a natural feature of New Jersey's land? What is a human feature?

4. Why is the Atlantic Ocean important to New Jersey's people?

5. What is New Jersey's nickname? What are its state symbols?

6. Name the first dinosaur ever found in America. Where was it found?

7. How did the glaciers shape our land?

THE TIME
11000 B.C.–A.D. 1758

PEOPLE TO KNOW
Paleo-Indians
Archaic people
Lenape Indians
Giovanni da Verrazano
James "Lone Bear" Revey

PLACES TO LOCATE
Delaware River
Europe
Indian Mills
Alloway
Cheesequake
Cinnaminson
Hackensack
Hoboken
Manahawkin
Manasquan
Manunkachunk
Neshanic
Passaic
Watchung

The First People

11000 B.C.
Paleo-Indians live over much of North America. They are the first people in the New Jersey region.

| 11000 B.C. | 9500 B.C. | 8000 B.C. | 6500 B.C. |

7000 B.C.
Archaic people live a more advanced lifestyle.

chapter

2

TERMS TO UNDERSTAND
sinew
artifact
archaeologist
colonist
clan
legend
origin
elder
sapling
quiver
immunity
reservation

900 A.D.
Lenape Indians begin to emerge as a distinctive group.

1758
The Indian reservation at Brotherton (now Indian Mills) is established for the Lenape people.

5000 B.C.	3500 B.C.	2000 B.C.	500 B.C.	1000 A.D.	1758 A.D.

1524
Giovanni da Verrazano is the first European to see Lenape Indians.

1730
Most Lenape Indians have left the New Jersey area.

Ancient Indians

THE FIRST PEOPLE WHO CAME TO WHAT we now call New Jersey were probably following wild animals. They hunted the animals for food. Mastodons, caribou, and wolves are animals that do well in cold climates. They roamed the northern parts of the continent, including New Jersey.

The ancient people found the land very different from the New Jersey we know today. There were glacial lakes and ponds. The ocean was almost a hundred miles from where it is now. The climate was very cold and wet. Because of the cold, only a few kinds of plants grew here.

Archaic people made tools from animal bones.

Paleo-Indians

The earliest people are called the Paleo-Indians. "Paleo" means ancient. The people hunted animals and gathered food from wild plants. The Paleo-Indians moved regularly in quest of the next meal. Paleo men hunted large animals with spears. Paleo women used bone needles to sew caribou hides together. The hides were used for clothes, blankets, and possibly as house coverings.

Archaic People

The Archaic people, who came after the Paleo-Indians, lived in a forest environment. They developed stone woodworking tools. They used the tools to chop down trees and make dugout canoes.

Archaic people hunted all kinds of animals, including birds, mammals, turtles, frogs, fish, and shellfish. All parts of the animal were used. The flesh was used as food. Hides were made into clothing, blankets, moccasins, and bags. Bones and antlers were used for tools, fishhooks, and whistles. *Sinews* and guts were used for sewing and binding skins to make clothing. Claws and teeth were sometimes made into necklaces and ornaments.

Nuts such as chestnuts and acorns were very important to the Archaic people because they could store them easily for use in the wintertime. They also ate many kinds of plants and certain roots. The people dried meat, fish, and other food for later use.

Archaeologists

The people who lived here long ago left no written records about their lives. However, they did leave behind clues that tell us how they lived. They left *artifacts* and other evidence, including burial sites, rock art, trash piles, and stone and ceramic pots. *Archaeologists* examine these clues to learn how and when the people lived.

Linking the past and the present

If you were suddenly to move and leave everything you own right where it is now, what could someone in a thousand years learn about you from your things? What could they not know? Remember that some objects like gold rings will preserve well, but other objects like iron or wood may rust and rot.

▶ Photo by David Blanchette

Archaeologists are scientists who study the things people of the past left behind. They must dig slowly and carefully. They try not to break tiny bones or artifacts that will help them learn about the people. Sometimes only a small brush is gentle enough to remove the dirt.

The First People

Lenape Indians

The name "Lenape" means "common" or "ordinary people."

"Lenapehoking" (Len-ah-pay-HAWK-ing) means the "land of the Lenape."

Different groups of people lived in New Jersey over many thousands of years. Some remained and others moved in or out. The Lenape Indians were here at least a thousand years ago. These were the same people who occupied the land when the European explorers and settlers arrived. Europeans called them the Delaware Indians because many of them lived along the Delaware River. The Lenape were on this land when the first explorers and *colonists* came to the region.

The Lenape Indians lived in small family groups called bands. They were part of the larger Algonquian (al-GON-kwin) Indian group. They spoke an Algonquian language.

The people usually lived near streams and rivers. Water was important because the people needed the fish and shellfish that lived in the streams. Streams and rivers were also the Indians' highways. They traveled in dugout canoes on the rivers. Traveling on water was faster than walking many miles on land. And, of course, the Lenape needed water for drinking, cooking, and washing.

Young boys learned to provide fish for the family.

Twenty or thirty people could live in a longhouse.

Making a Home

The Lenape used *saplings*, tree bark, reeds, and grass mats to make wigwams and longhouses. Saplings were thin young trees. They were curved and tied together to make the frame of the house and roof. They were covered with bark to keep out the rain and snow. Small openings in the roof let the smoke escape from the fires inside the home.

Wigwams were small and round. One or two families could live in one.

A Step-by-Step Wigwam

1 To build a wigwam, the people cut down young trees called **saplings**. They trimmed off the branches. Then they dug holes in the ground. They put saplings in the holes. This held the saplings in place.

2 They bent the saplings over, then lashed them together with cord, vines, or animal skins. This made a frame for the wigwam.

3 Finally, they covered the frame with bark or mats made of grasses and reeds. They left a door and a hole in the top so the smoke from the fire could escape.

▲ Photos by Suzanne Chapelle, Courtesy of the Irvine Nature Center

Lenape Families

Family was very important to the Lenape. When a man married a woman, he often went to live with her family.

Every Lenape belonged to a *clan*. There were three clans: the turtle, wolf, and turkey. In order to be married, a man and woman had to be from different clans. If a woman was from the turtle clan, her husband would have to be from the wolf or turkey clan. Children belonged to the same clan as their mother.

Older people held a special place in the clan. They were respected for their wisdom and age. Children listened to stories and *legends* from their grandparents. This was one way history was passed down from generation to generation. *Elders* were older people. Some elders used healing plants to treat wounds and cure illnesses.

The Lenape needed to be very strong. For this reason, mothers would dunk their babies in a cold stream every day. In the winter, they rubbed them with snow. Children might be scolded from time to time. Cold water sometimes was thrown in their faces if they did not behave. Children were taught to be respectful and to never bring shame on their family.

Mothers carried their babies on cradleboards.

When a person died, people did not say his or her name again because it would make the family sad. Favorite things and food were placed in the graves for use in the next world.

Marriage and Divorce

Lenape girls usually got married when they were about fifteen years old. Boys were a few years older. If a young man wanted to marry a young woman, he would give a piece of meat to her family. By doing this, he showed himself to be a good hunter. In return, she offered him some food she had cooked. This showed that she would be a good wife. If they both agreed, they would be married.

Lenape women cooked the food, wove baskets, and made other basic items.

Marriages usually lasted, but people sometimes got divorced. If a woman wanted to divorce her husband, she put all his things outside the house to let him know that he should leave. If a man wanted a divorce, he would leave his wife's house. The children stayed with the mother. If there was a divorce, the people could marry again.

Lenape Names

Children often died very young. For that reason, they were not given a real name until they were four or five years old. Instead, they were given a nickname. When the child was older, a special person called a "name-giver" was asked to dream or think up a name for the child. This was a private name between the person and the spirits. Other people still called the person by his or her nickname.

In those days, children of most cultures often died from disease, starvation, poor diets, and lack of medical care.

The Meanings of Names	
Lel-pooch-way	He Who Walks Swiftly
Ee-heh-sung-wes	He Who Hunts Weasels
Ma-eh-hu-mund	One Who Gathers Things
Neta-wata-wes	Skilled Advisor
Shingas	Swamp Person
Tu-mak-way-tut	Little Beaver
Way-auchay-lingaut	Bright Eyes

Sharing the Work

Lenape women and girls were in charge of taking care of the home and meals. They gathered plants, roots, and berries; carried firewood; and cooked the meals. The women also made all the pots, baskets, and clothing for the family. They used animal skins and furs to make clothing, moccasins, and blankets.

Lenape men proved themselves to be good husbands by hunting for the family.

Lenape men and boys chopped down trees, built the houses, and made canoes. They did all the hunting and fishing to provide the family with food. Hunting was hard work. The hunter might spend all day without killing a bird or animal. When he did get an animal, he carried it home. Then his wife skinned it and fixed the meat.

No part of the animal was wasted. The meat, heart, and liver were eaten. The bone and fat were used to make soup. The skin was used for blankets and clothing. The bones and teeth were used to make tools.

Games and Celebrations

There was a lot of work to do, but the people also played games. Boys practiced their aim with bows and arrows. The games were fun and they helped to sharpen hunting skills. For example, in the hoop and pole game, the "hunter" tried to throw a pole through a moving hoop. This helped him to hit a moving target. Wrestling was a common game of skill. Children had races and contests to test their speed and strength. Girls played with dolls. They dressed them in costumes.

Music and dancing were important as well. Drums were made from a dried animal skin stretched over a hollowed-out log. Rattles and whistles were made from bird bones and shells. Telling stories and legends and singing were also ways to have fun.

A Spiritual People

The Lenape believed that everything had a spirit, including the air, fire, water, trees, animals, birds, insects, and stones. The people asked spirits to help them have a good hunt or to win wars. They believed that the spirits of certain plants could make them well again.

American Indians lived close to nature. The ground under their feet was more than just grass, rock, and earth. The sun in the sky was more than just a ball of fire. They wanted to see and feel and touch the earth every day.

Sharing was important. They said that the land people farmed and hunted on and all rivers and lakes they fished in belonged to everyone in the group.

Vision Quest

Illustrations by Ray Cornia

When a Lenape boy was twelve or thirteen years old, he went on a journey called a vision quest. This was how he found his own guardian spirit.

The boy went out alone to the mountains or forest. He went without food or water. When he was scared and hungry, he prayed for his guardian spirit to come and protect him. The spirit might appear as an eagle, wolf, beetle, or some other sign from nature.

From then on, his guardian spirit would protect him in times of illness, danger, or distress.

The First People

41

Legends and Myths

American Indians had legends that told their history. They were stories that explained how the tribe came to be. Legends also answered questions in nature, such as why the owl stays up at night or why the fox is so sly. They told of animals and spirits coming to teach or help the people. In the legends, animals were often used to teach children about how to be strong and good. Legends were usually told during the winter months when the people stayed indoors around a fire.

Legends were stories told out loud from memory. They were passed from one generation to the next.

The Boy and the Squirrel

Long ago it is said a boy went hunting. He carried his bow, and on his back he carried a quiver. He went to a big woods. He was hunting squirrels. Suddenly he saw a squirrel on a branch chewing on an acorn. He raised his bow and shot at the squirrel, but he missed him.

The squirrel ran down the tree, and into a hole in the tree. The boy began to gather up stones and stuff them into the hole. Then he ran home and told his parents. When he finished eating, he went to the big woods to look for the squirrel. When he got to the tree, he heard the squirrel singing. This is what the squirrel was singing:

"Little boy, little boy, you can never starve me to death, little boy."

Then when that boy grew up and became a man he used that song in the Big House Church as his vision song.

—as told by Nora Thompson Dean, 1969

European Contact

Soon after the New World was discovered, European explorers started coming to North America. Italian explorer Giovanni da Verrazano was the first European to meet the Lenape Indians. Here is how he described the Lenape people:

> *These people are the most beautiful . . . They are taller than we are; they are a bronze color . . . their face is clearcut; the hair is long and black, and they take great care in decorating it; the eyes are black and alert, and their manner is sweet and gentle.*

Other explorers began to trade with the Lenape. Europeans brought beads, mirrors, iron knives, axes, cloth, and other items the Indians had never seen. The Indians traded animal skins and furs, corn, and even land.

Europeans also brought diseases to the New World. They gave the American Indians illnesses they had never known before. The diseases, including smallpox, measles, and chicken pox, killed many Lenape Indians. They had no *immunity* against the new diseases.

As more explorers and colonists arrived in the New World, they wanted American Indian land. Sometimes they bought and traded for the land. But often, they simply forced the Indians off the land. Gradually, the Lenape were pushed back to the Delaware River. Later the settlers wanted that land too. The Indians then had to move even farther west.

Indian Reservation

The first and only Indian *reservation* in New Jersey was called Brotherton in the hopes that all men living there would treat each other as brothers. In time, most Lenape moved to Oklahoma, Wisconsin, and Canada. A small number still live in New Jersey.

What do you think?

How did the European explorers change the life of the Lenape? In what ways were the changes good? In what ways were they harmful?

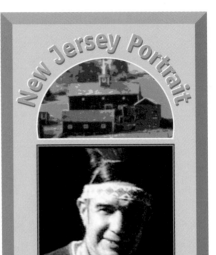
James "Lone Bear" Revey
1924–1998

James Revey belonged to the "Sand Hill" band of Lenape Indians who once occupied parts of Monmouth County. He served in World War II and attended Bacone College in Oklahoma. Mr. Revey earned his living by making authentic Indian arts and crafts. Some of his headdresses were used in such Broadway plays as *Singing in the Rain.* Lone Bear's real mission in life was to preserve the memory of his people. He visited fourth-grade students throughout northern New Jersey. He told them about his Lenape ancestors and showed them the beautiful ceremonial garments his grandmother had made for him. His beaded moccasins and beaded vest are shown on this page.

Activity

Bury a Time Capsule

Would you like someone in the future to uncover things you've left behind? What could they learn about your lifestyle?

1. Collect a bunch of things that describe what your life is like now. Your class picture, a ticket stub from a sporting event or movie, and an empty box of your favorite cereal are all good things to put in a time capsule. Add pictures you've drawn of things you like (and don't like). You could even make a tape of your favorite songs.

2. Put everything into a waterproof container with a tight lid. Label the container with the date you made it. Decorate it for fun. Be sure to use a container that will not rust or decay.

3. Bury your time capsule in your yard for future people to find. What might they learn about you? Will their lives be similar to yours?

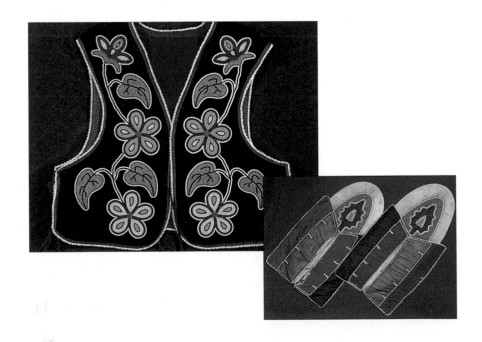

Naming New Jersey Places

Do you know that many places in New Jersey have American Indian names? Here are some of the names and what they mean. Are any of these places near you?

Alloway	"more"
Cheesequake	"land which has been cleared"
Cinnaminson	"rocky place of fish"
Hackensack	"place of sharp ground"
Hoboken	"tobacco pipe"
Manahawkin	"where the land slopes"
Manasquan	"place to gather grass"
Manunkachunk	"where the hills are clustered"
Neshanic	"two creeks"
Passaic	"valley"
Watchung	"hilly place"

Chapter 2 Review

1. How did the first people in New Jersey get food?
2. What things from nature did the Lenape Indians use to make their homes?
3. What are the three Lenape clans?
4. How did a Lenape Indian get a name?
5. Why did the Lenape Indians tell legends?
6. What is a vision quest? Who went on one, and why?
7. How did European explorers and colonists get American Indian lands?

Geography Tie-In

1. Give some examples of how the Indians used the land to meet their needs.
2. What part did the Delaware River play in the lives of the Lenape Indians?

THE TIME
1492–1660

PEOPLE TO KNOW
Marco Polo
Christopher Columbus
John Cabot
Amerigo Vespucci
Henry Hudson
Robert Juet
Giovanni da Verrazano
Cornelius Mey
Michael Pauw
Penelope Stout
Johan Printz
Peter Stuyvesant

PLACES TO LOCATE
Europe
Asia
Africa
The Indies
Portugal
Cape of Good Hope
Italy
England
The Netherlands
Newfoundland
Sandy Hook
France
Cape May
Camden
Jersey City
Sweden
Finland
Swedesboro

Exploration and European Settlement

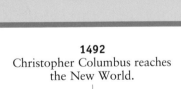

1492
Christopher Columbus reaches
the New World.

1524
Giovanni da Verrazano explores
the New Jersey coastline.

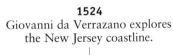

timeline of events   1480   1500   1520   1540

1497
John Cabot claims land along the
coast of North America for England.

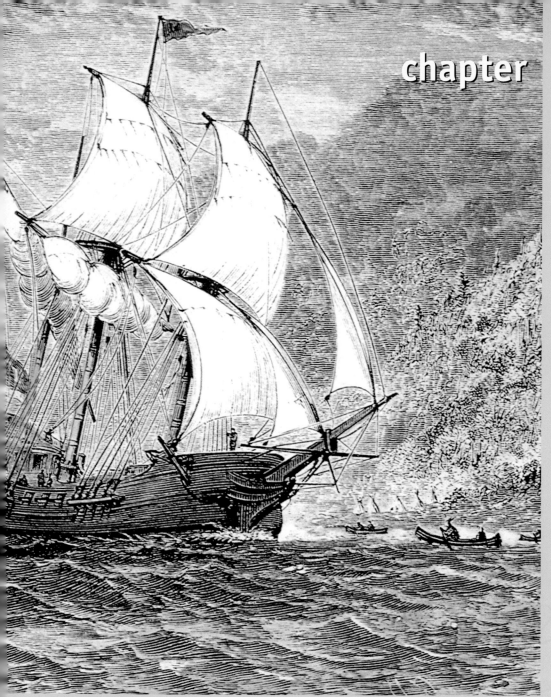

TERMS TO UNDERSTAND
merchant
caravan
luxury
necessity
voyage
circa
strait
deceive
anchor
permanent
colony
patroon
mistreat
massacre

On his ship the Half Moon, *Henry Hudson explored the New Jersey coastline.* (Photo from North Wind)

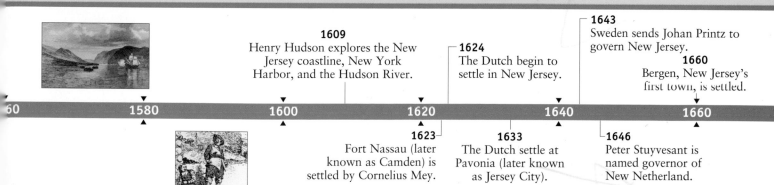

1609
Henry Hudson explores the New Jersey coastline, New York Harbor, and the Hudson River.

1624
The Dutch begin to settle in New Jersey.

1643
Sweden sends Johan Printz to govern New Jersey.

1660
Bergen, New Jersey's first town, is settled.

60   1580   1600   1620   1640   1660

1623
Fort Nassau (later known as Camden) is settled by Cornelius Mey.

1633
The Dutch settle at Pavonia (later known as Jersey City).

1646
Peter Stuyvesant is named governor of New Netherland.

European Contact

BY THE EARLY 1400s, people from Europe had been trading with people in Asia and Africa for almost 1,500 years. Europeans brought fine rugs; silk; spices such as cinnamon, pepper, and nutmeg; and other new and exciting things to Europe from Asia.

Marco Polo, an Italian businessman, traveled to Asia and the Indies and brought back things such as paper, coal, and gunpowder. Following him were other **merchants** who were willing to make the long and dangerous trip. They bought items that sold for very high prices in Europe. Europeans really liked these things and wanted more of them.

The only problem was that the overland trade routes were very long and dangerous to travel. There were mountains and deserts to cross. All too often, robbers would attack **caravans**.

The spices found in Asia and the Indies were not just a *luxury*. They were a *necessity*. Since there were no refrigerators, spices were needed to keep food from spoiling. Some spices were even more valuable than gold.

Merchants used ships and animals to transport goods from Asia to Europe.

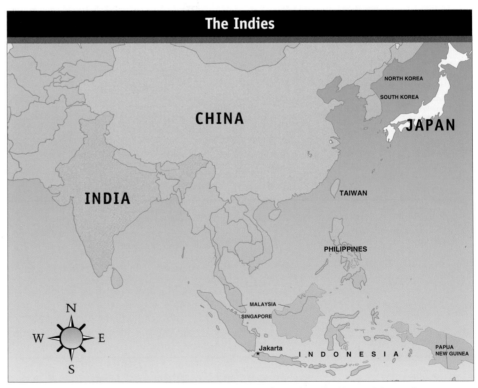

The Indies

NORTH KOREA

SOUTH KOREA

JAPAN

CHINA

INDIA

TAIWAN

PHILIPPINES

MALAYSIA

SINGAPORE

Jakarta   I N D O N E S I A   PAPUA NEW GUINEA

N W E S

The lands in eastern Asia were known as the Indies. This region included India, Japan, China, and the surrounding islands. Locate these places on the map.

▲ Photo from North Wind

Some countries, such as Portugal, tried to send ships around Africa. But that was very dangerous because of the violent storms around the Cape of Good Hope.

Trade was growing rapidly in Europe. Europeans were looking for a new route to Asia.

Christopher Columbus

Young Christopher Columbus used to sit on the pier of his sea-port home of Genoa, Italy, and watch the ships coming into the harbor from faraway places. Columbus talked with the sailors about their adventures.

Soon he was old enough to sail on those trading ships. One day his ship was wrecked off the coast of Portugal. He lived there for a while and got a job as a sailor and a mapmaker.

Columbus believed Asia and the Indies could be reached by sailing west from Portugal. His plan was to sail west to reach the East. He didn't know North and South America were in between. For many years he tried to get someone to listen to his plan. King Ferdinand and Queen Isabella of Spain wanted Columbus to spread the Catholic religion to the people in Asia. They also wanted an ocean route to Asia. They agreed to give him the ships he needed to make the **voyage**. With his three ships, he set sail.

On October 12, 1492, Columbus reached what he thought were the Indies. He really had reached an island near Florida. After claiming the land for Spain, he named the island San Salvador, which is Spanish for "Holy Savior." He named the people he found living there "Indians," since he believed he was in the Indies.

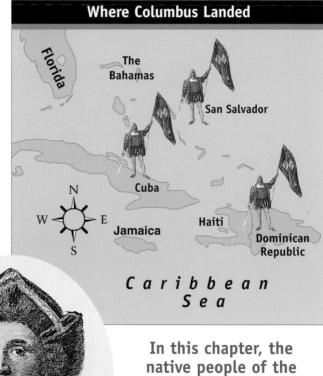

Christopher Columbus

Where Columbus Landed

In this chapter, the native people of the United States are called Indians. Early European explorers and settlers called them Indians. Today, they are usually referred to as American Indians, Native Americans, or Native People.

John Cabot

Columbus and his crew never knew they had found a new continent. They thought they had landed in Asia. Only five years after Columbus's voyage to the New World, English leaders were also looking for a shorter route to the Indies. They sent an Italian explorer by the name of John Cabot on that mission.

Cabot set sail with a crew of eighteen men. They landed on the shore of North America, but they, too, thought they were in Asia. Cabot returned to England, but he later made another trip to America. He did not find wealthy cities or spices.

Because of John Cabot's discovery, England claimed a great amount of land in the New World. It was along the East Coast that the United States would have its beginning.

John Cabot

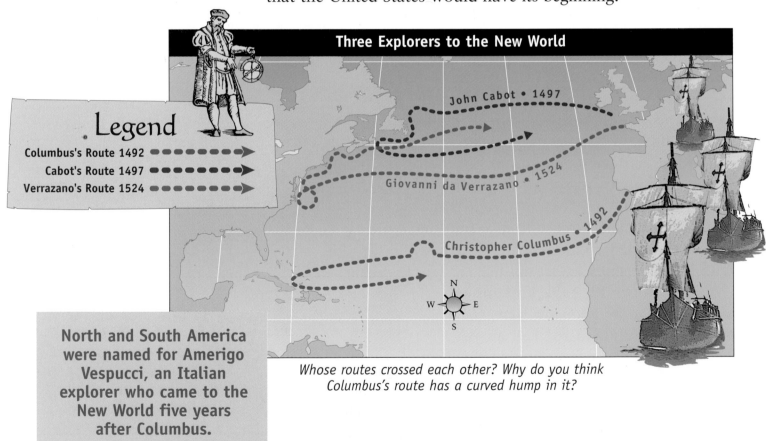

Three Explorers to the New World

John Cabot • 1497

Giovanni da Verrazano • 1524

Christopher Columbus • 1492

Legend

Columbus's Route 1492 ●●●●●●➤
Cabot's Route 1497 ●●●●●●➤
Verrazano's Route 1524 ●●●●●●➤

N
W—E
S

Whose routes crossed each other? Why do you think Columbus's route has a curved hump in it?

North and South America were named for Amerigo Vespucci, an Italian explorer who came to the New World five years after Columbus.

Henry Hudson

In the early 1600s, the Dutch were looking for a route to the Far East. The Dutch East India Company hired an English sea captain by the name of Henry Hudson to sail west and find a shorter way. Hudson set sail from Holland in a wooden ship called the *Half Moon*. He headed towards the northern seas.

Twenty men, some English and some Dutch, made up the crew. They constantly argued with Hudson and themselves. In May, when the ship was off the coast of Norway, they headed into some very stormy weather. The Dutch sailors wanted to return home.

Robert Juet, one of Hudson's officers, kept a journal. It described many of the things that happened on the voyage. He described the Dutch crew as "an ugly lot." An English officer by the name of John Coleman wrote, "I hope these . . . men know the sea. Looking at their . . . bellies, I fear they may think more . . . of eating than sailing."

A few months later, Hudson put aside his plan to find a water route through North America. He headed south. He reached the coast of Virginia and then headed north again, sailing along the East Coast. Soon he passed the mouth of the Delaware River and dropped anchor off the coast of what we call Sandy Hook, New Jersey.

A Rough Beginning

For six days, Hudson and his crew explored the area. The Indians were very friendly. They gave gifts of tobacco to everyone. Hudson in return gave them knives and beads. The Europeans were fascinated by the Indians' deerskin clothing, corn bread, fine furs, and copper pipes. The copper pipes really got the attention of Hudson and his crew. That metal was also used in many ways in Europe. It was made into coins, pots, and other items.

The beautiful land with its "pleasant grasse and flowers and goodly trees" impressed the explorers. Hudson wrote that these people are "very civil" [polite]. But, Juet wrote in his journal, "we did not trust them."

New Jersey Portrait

Giovanni da Verrazano
circa 1480–1527

The first European ever to see and possibly land on the shores of New Jersey was Giovanni da Verrazano. He was an Italian explorer who was sent by France to explore the New World. Some people believe that at one time he was a pirate. He landed near Sandy Hook. He and his men explored the New Jersey coastline and the Upper New York Bay. He was looking for a *strait* (water route) that would go from the Atlantic Ocean to the Pacific Ocean. Verrazano did not find the strait he was looking for. What he did find was land that stretched from Newfoundland to the Carolinas. The Verrazano Narrows Bridge that joins Staten Island to New York was named after him.

Relations Turn Sour

At first, the Indians and explorers got along well. But, in some cases, there were bad feelings on both sides. Some people believe that the bad behavior of the European crew and how they treated the Indians caused them to turn from friendly to angry. Indians attacked and killed some of Hudson's crew members. That night Juet wrote in his journal, the crew "kept a careful watch."

Soon the Indians and Hudson's crew were trading with each other again. Juet wrote, "two great canoes full of natives come on board in an attempt to **deceive** us, pretended interest in buying knives. But we . . . took two of them prisoners." Later that day, two more were taken prisoner. One jumped overboard and the others were released that night.

New World Treasures

Hudson sailed up the Hudson River. The next day he gave orders for the *Half Moon* to be **anchored** off the coast of Manhattan. He wrote about land filled with forests and beavers and other animals that could be trapped for their beautiful fur. The rivers and ocean were filled with fish. Hudson also reported that the people were friendly.

Hudson's report of the land inspired many trappers and adventurers to come to the New World. At first, many Dutch people were interested in beaver fur and gold. They were not planning on establishing **permanent** colonies and settlements. The Dutch started by setting up trading posts in New Jersey.

Hudson's Third Voyage, 1609

Gulf of St. Lawrence

Hudson River

Sandy Hook
Barnegat Bay
Delaware Bay

Atlantic Ocean

N
W E
S

Describe what you think Hudson and his crew saw and heard as they sailed up the New Jersey coast. What do you think they would see and hear today?

▲ Photo from North Wind

Hudson's Half Moon *traveled along the Hudson River.*

The New Jersey Adventure

Explorers and trappers traveled along the New Jersey coastline, on the rivers, and in and out of the bays. Today, ships of all kinds travel along the coastline, bringing goods in and out of New Jersey. The waterways are still important.

Early Settlements

The land Henry Hudson explored was called New Netherland. It included parts of New Jersey and New York. New Amsterdam was the capital. It later became part of New York.

A Dutch explorer, Captain Cornelius Mey, explored the Delaware Bay area. He named the peninsula at the southern tip of New Jersey for himself. Although it's spelled differently today, Cape May reminds us of the captain's early exploration. A trading post called Fort Nassau (later known as Camden) was started. A year later, Mey returned with a few families and started a *colony* on what is now Burlington Island.

Moving to the New World

The Dutch West India Company was put in charge of running New Netherland. They were having a hard time getting people to settle the new colony. They came up with a plan called the *patroon* system. A person became a patroon by having the company give him a large piece of land in New Netherland. The land was called a patroonship.

A patroon promised the company to bring at least fifty settlers to work the land in the colony. A patroon named Michael Pauw was given land near what is now Jersey City. He named the land after himself. He called it Pavonia. The only problem was that he could not find fifty people to come to live and settle on his patroonship. He had to give the land back to the Dutch West India Company. Only two houses had been built, but some of the settlers did not return to Holland. They decided to stay and make a new life for themselves.

High Fashion

The beaver hat was the reason our land was explored so much by the trappers. These hats were the fashion for European gentlemen. Hat makers could hardly keep up with all the hats people wanted. People wanted fur for other reasons, too. It became popular for both ladies and gentlemen to wear fox, otter, and other animal fur on coat collars, sleeves, gloves, and boots.

The trappers in Europe had killed all the beavers there. When they learned that the land around New Jersey had beavers, they came here to trap them.

A Terrible Massacre

Some of the Dutch were beginning to *mistreat* the Indians. The leader of New Amsterdam ordered his soldiers to drive away the Indians in a small village near Pavonia. One night eighty of his soldiers *massacred* about eighty sleeping Indian men, women, and children. Indians attacked settlers for almost two years before peace was reached. The Lenape were friendly people. But, if they were mistreated they could become fierce fighters.

What do you think?

When the Europeans came into the New Jersey region they changed the lifestyle of the Indians. Do you think the Indians changed the lifestyle of the Europeans?

Europeans introduced many new diseases to the Indians. Smallpox and measles caused thousands of deaths. The Indians had no way to protect themselves from these diseases.

◄ Photo from North Wind

This is how New Amsterdam looked in the mid 1600s.

Penelope Stout

When the colony of New Amsterdam was less than twenty years old, a Dutch family left their home in Holland and sailed for America. During a raging storm, their ship was wrecked off the coast of Sandy Hook. A young bride named Penelope Van Princis and her husband were part of the group of survivors. Her husband was very sick and the two of them struggled off the beach and ended up on the edge of a forest.

They were found by a group of Indians who were at war with the white settlers. They killed Penelope's husband. Thinking that she was also dead, they left Penelope next to her husband. She wandered in the woods until she found a hollowed-out tree trunk and made it her home. She survived on what she found on and around the tree trunk.

After a few days another group of Indian people found her. They fed her and treated her wounds. She worked with the women pounding corn, cooking, making pottery and clothes, clearing the land, and planting.

Soon word reached a small village that a woman was living in a nearby Indian village and that she was being held as a slave. A group of men went to the village. The Indian who had carried the sick and dying Penelope into the village asked Penelope if she wanted to stay with them or leave. Penelope decided to go to New Amsterdam. Everyone at the Indian village was very sad to see her go, but they respected her choice.

Dutch families were beginning to live closer and closer together. The first town in New Jersey was named Bergen. Bergen later became Jersey City.

Swedish and Finnish Immigrants

Sweden and Finland are countries in Europe. The King of Sweden wanted to start a colony on the Delaware River. He sent a group of colonists to America to start the colony of Fort Christina. It was named after his wife, the Queen of Sweden. Today it is known as Wilmington, Delaware.

Two years later a very large piece of land was purchased from the Indians in southern New Jersey. The town of Swedesboro was started. The whole area was called New Sweden. The settlers wanted to trade with the Indians for furs. The colony only had ninety-eight people. Its small population made it open to attack from other countries.

Johan Printz was sent to govern New Sweden. He was a very large man. He stood about seven feet tall and weighed about 400 pounds. The Indians called him "Big Tub." Many people thought he was too strict and treated both the colonists and Indians too roughly.

Johan Printz was the government leader of New Sweden.

What type of mood do you think Peter Stuyvesant is in? He is the one in the red jacket waving the cane.

Peter Stuyvesant and New Netherland

A new director general was sent to New Amsterdam. He was a very strict leader by the name of Peter Stuyvesant.

Stuyvesant sent a messenger to Johan Printz telling him to surrender New Sweden to the Dutch. Johan Printz surrendered. Director General Stuyvesant gave the Swedes and Finns a choice of either staying and cooperating with the Dutch government or returning to their own countries. Most of the Swedes and Finns decided to stay.

Activity

Primary Sources Reveal History

History is not only about what happened in the ancient past, it is about what happened last month and last year.

A historian is a person who studies the past. When we study history it helps to think like a historian. Ask yourself these questions as you read: What happened? Who took part in it? Why did it happen? When did it happen?

Let's start with the first question: What happened? To determine what really happened in the past, you need evidence. There are two types of sources you can go to—primary sources and secondary sources.

Primary sources are records made by people who were there at the time. Primary means "first" or a first-hand account. A Lenape basket is a primary source. Robert Juet's diary is a primary source.

Secondary sources are something written or made by someone who was *not* there at the time. A newspaper article or a book written at a later time are secondary sources. A modern painting of Columbus's ships is a secondary source. They are second-hand accounts.

On a separate piece of paper, number from one to six. Put a P (for primary source) or an S (for secondary source) for each item.

1. A film made today about European explorers.

2. Journals and ship logs written by early Dutch sailors.

3. A letter written by an early New Jersey settler.

4. A modern copy of an old rifle.

5. A copper pipe from a Lenape Indian.

6. A ship built to look like the *Half Moon*.

Activity

An Explorer's Journal

Step into a time machine and open the door to 400 years ago. You are an explorer. You travel by land and by water. You walk, ride horses, and sail in boats. You travel without maps.

Write a daily journal of your adventures just like Robert Juet of the *Half Moon*. Be sure to include where you are going, who is with you, and how you are traveling. Describe what you see, hear, smell, and taste. Write about people and animals you see. Write about your adventures!

Chapter 3 Review

1. Name some of the things that the early Europeans brought back to Europe from the Indies.

2. What made the journey to the Indies very dangerous?

3. Why was Columbus's discovery important for the world?

4. Name the great "treasure" John Cabot and his crew found off the northeast coast of America.

5. What was Giovanni da Verrazano looking for? Did he ever find it?

6. Where did Henry Hudson step ashore in New Jersey? What exciting news did he bring back to Holland?

7. Describe how a patroon system works.

Geography Tie-In

1. At one time, parts of New Jersey were called New Netherland and New Sweden. Can you explain why?

THE TIME
1664–1763

PEOPLE TO KNOW
King Charles of England
Duke of York
Richard Nicolls
Lord John Berkeley
Sir George Carteret
Philip Carteret
Robert Treat
William Penn
William Kidd
Edward Teach
Queen Anne of England
William Franklin
Lewis Morris

PLACES TO LOCATE
Massachusetts
Virginia
Long Island
Passaic River
Newark
Woodbridge
Piscataway
Hope
Elizabeth
Shrewsbury
Middletown
Salem
Greenwich
Little Egg Harbor
Delaware Water Gap
Burlington
Perth Amboy

timeline of events

1664
Peter Stuyvesant surrenders New Netherland to the English.
Richard Nicholls is named governor of New York.
The Duke of York gives land in Albania to Lord Berkeley
and Sir George Carteret.

1666 Puritans settle Newark.

1660   1670   1680   1690   1700

1676
New Jersey is divided into
East and West Jersey.

1665
Philip Carteret becomes the governor of New Jersey.
Immigrants begin coming to New Jersey.
The Quakers write the *Concessions and Agreements*.

1702
Queen Anne unites
East and West Jersey.

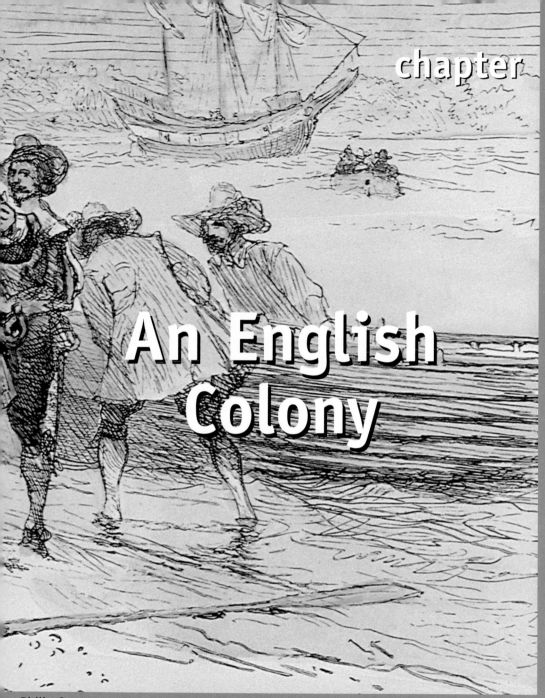

chapter 4

An English Colony

TERMS TO UNDERSTAND
empire
sacrifice
entice
fertile
proprietors
govern
assembly
tax
guarantee
freight
descendant
royal
rival
ally
barracks

Philip Carteret arrives to take over the colony of New Netherland. (Illustration from North Wind)

710   1720   1730   1740   1750   1760   1770

1763
William Franklin becomes governor.

1738
Lewis Morris becomes the first governor
of the united New Jersey.

1754–1763
French and Indian War

The Colony of New Jersey

THE ENGLISH PEOPLE WERE ATTRACTED by the natural resources in the New World. They wanted beaver fur and other things. They were also interested in starting colonies. They wanted to send people to live permanently in the New World. That way, England would be in charge of more land and more people.

By the middle of the 1600s, there were more English settlers in America than Dutch or Swedes. England had colonies from Massachusetts to Virginia and was looking to control all the land in between. England did not want the Dutch or Swedes to be in the way of making her *empire* even larger.

The English felt that they had a right to the land because John Cabot had claimed the region for England over one hundred years before Henry Hudson claimed it for Holland. With

Governor Stuyvesant sent his assistant to surrender New Netherland.

that in mind, King Charles of England gave the colony of New Netherland to his brother, who was called the Duke of York.

The Duke of York sent his good friend Richard Nicolls and four ships filled with soldiers to New Netherland. They demanded that the Dutch leader, Peter Stuyvesant, surrender the colony to them. There was no fighting. The takeover happened peacefully. Many of the colonists believed that to be ruled by England would be better than to be ruled by Holland and its strict governor. Peter Stuyvesant quietly left with his army and sailed back to Holland.

Dutch settlers came from a country called the Netherlands. Holland is part of the Netherlands.

Settlers Come for Land

The English allowed the Dutch, Swedish, and Finnish settlers to remain on the land as long as they promised to obey English laws. Many of them stayed. This was their home. They had made great *sacrifices* to settle the area.

In honor of the Duke of York, Nicolls named the land west of the Hudson River *Albania*. The name Albania was chosen because the Duke of York was also the Duke of Albany in England.

Nicolls realized that he needed settlers in order to make a strong English colony. He came up with a plan to *entice* settlers to come to Albania. They would be able to buy land from the

Photo from North Wind

Settlers came to places like New Germantown, New Jersey.

American Indians at a very low price. They would have more freedom than they had in their own countries. They would be able to make their own laws.

The land in Albania was very *fertile*. It had plenty of freshwater streams and lakes, thick forests, and an excellent climate. Before anyone knew it, settlers were coming from all over. A large group came from Long Island and settled in what is now Union County. Land near the Raritan Bay was settled by a second group of settlers from Long Island.

The American Indians were given things such as metal tools, pots, cloth, guns, and gunpowder in exchange for their land. But the Indians thought they were only allowing the settlers to use the land. They believed that everyone should share the land. It belonged to the Great Spirit or Creator. They did not realize that they were giving up their land for good.

Carteret and Berkeley

The Duke of York gave the land between the Hudson and Delaware Rivers to his close friends Lord John Berkeley and Sir George Carteret. They were called the *proprietors*, or owners, of the colony. Lord Berkeley was given the western half of New Jersey and Sir George Carteret was given the eastern half. This was a tremendous amount of land to control.

Since Berkeley and Carteret both lived in England, someone had to *govern* the land. They agreed to send Philip Carteret, a cousin, to do the job.

Philip Carteret came to the colony and told Richard Nicholls that he was the new governor. Richard Nicholls had no idea that he was to be replaced. He wrote a very angry letter to the Duke of York in England. The Duke of York gave Nicholls Staten Island to replace the land he had lost.

Almost as soon as he stepped ashore, Philip Carteret announced to the settlers that they would be allowed to practice the religion of their choice. They also would be allowed to come together and make their own laws. They could elect a group called an *assembly* to make the laws. That was the good news.

The bad news was that the settlers now had to pay a *tax* on their property. They never had to do this before. The tax money would be collected once a year and was to go to the proprietors. The settlers were not happy with this. They felt that they owned the land since they had bought it from the Indians.

Activity

Naming New Jersey

The land we call New Jersey has had many different names. It was called New Netherland, Albania, and then New Jersey. All of the names came from European places.

Research the name of your city or town. What does it mean? Where did it come from? Was your city named after a famous person?

Where did Swedesboro get its name?

▶ Photo from North Wind

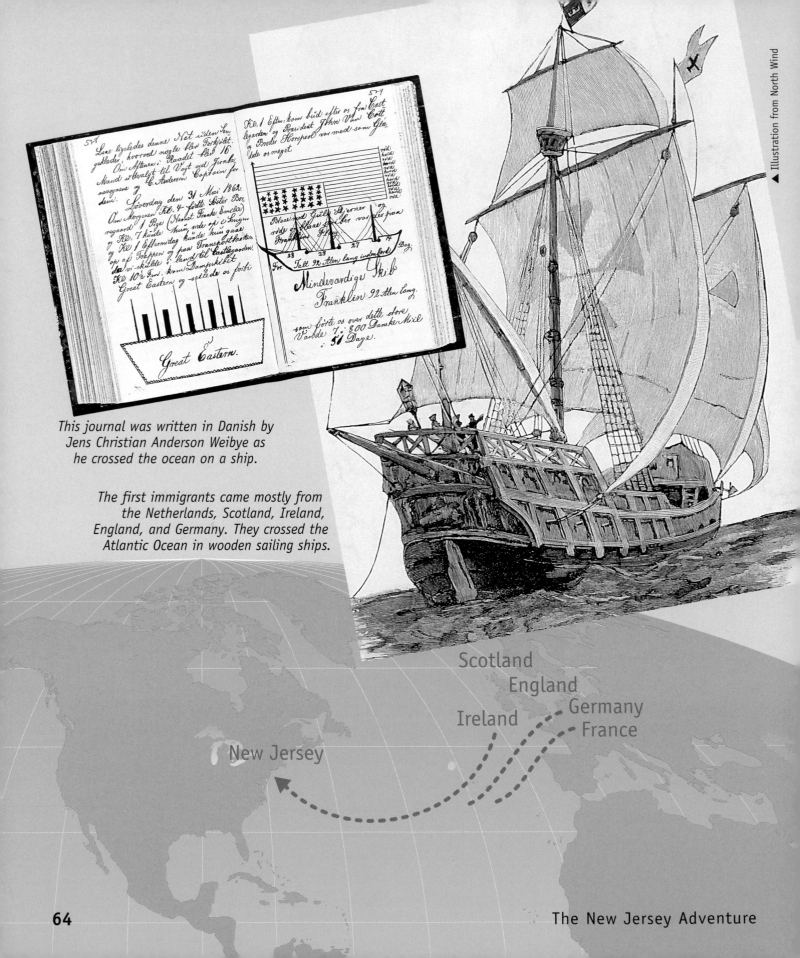

This journal was written in Danish by Jens Christian Anderson Weibye as he crossed the ocean on a ship.

The first immigrants came mostly from the Netherlands, Scotland, Ireland, England, and Germany. They crossed the Atlantic Ocean in wooden sailing ships.

Scotland

England

Ireland

Germany

France

New Jersey

The New Jersey Adventure

New Jersey Settlers

Dutch Settlers

There were many Dutch families moving into New Jersey from New York at this time. They settled in Bergen and Somerset Counties. Traditions and customs from their old country were important to them. Most farmers worked to get more land, which they divided up among their sons. African slaves were often brought to help work on the farms.

Scotch-Irish Settlers

People from Scotland and Ireland moved into the hills of Somerset, Morris, and Sussex Counties. People came from Scotland and Ireland because of the very high taxes they had to pay in their countries.

German Settlers

The Germans came a little later and settled in Hunterdon and Sussex Counties. They were excellent farmers.

French Settlers

A group from France called the Huguenots came because they were being put in prison and killed for their religious beliefs.

English Settlers and Others

English settlers started many farms and towns in the southern counties of New Jersey. Many other settlers came from other colonies such as Massachusetts and Connecticut.

Welsh, Belgian, French, and African settlers were soon found in all the counties. A group called the Quakers came to New Jersey to worship as they believed.

New Jersey has twenty-one counties. Locate the counties where each group settled.

Religious Immigrants

Puritans

The Puritans wanted to purify the Church of England. Can you see how they got their name?

Many immigrants came to the New World to have the freedom to practice their religion. In England, some people were unhappy with the Church of England (also called the Anglican Church). Everyone was expected to worship in Anglican churches and pay taxes to support the Church. Those who did not were considered disloyal to England. There was no religious freedom in England or anywhere else in Europe at that time.

A group called the Puritans did not like the Church of England. They met with trouble when they tried to live their own beliefs. Most Puritans wanted to change the Church of England by staying within it. But a small group wanted to separate from the Church. They thought the Church could not be changed. They were known as Separatists. This small group became the Pilgrims who settled in Massachusetts.

In 1666, Robert Treat brought thirty Puritan families to start a town along the Passaic River. This is now the city of Newark. One year later the population of Newark was about 350. Other Puritans from Massachusetts and New Hampshire soon followed and started the towns of Woodbridge and Piscataway.

What do you think?

The word "pilgrim" means someone who wanders. Why do you think this name was given to the Separatists?

The Moravians came from Germany and founded some towns in New Jersey.

Moravians

Another religious group called the Moravians started the town of Hope. They were from Germany. Many of the Moravians shared their Christian beliefs with the American Indians. Some Indians became Christians. Moravian settlers from Long Island were responsible for starting Elizabethtown, which would later become the towns of Elizabeth, Shrewsbury, and Middletown.

William Penn was a Quaker who started Philadelphia. He bought land from the Indians. He was known for treating the Indians with great respect.

Quakers

The Quakers were another religious group that broke apart from the Church of England. They came to Pennsylvania and New Jersey to practice their own beliefs. Quakers believed in the basic human goodness of every person. They strove to be simple in all things. Their dress was simple. Their meetings did not follow an organized pattern.

Lord Berkeley sold his western part of New Jersey to the Quakers. When the Quakers bought the land they became the proprietors. Soon the towns of Salem, which means "peace," and Greenwich were added to the map of New Jersey.

The Quaker settlers wrote up a set of rules called the *Concessions and Agreements* to help govern themselves. This set of rules *guaranteed* their religious freedom. It also listed rights and responsibilities that everyone shared.

Linking the past and the present

Many people came to New Jersey so they could live their religion. Is there religious freedom in New Jersey today? Is religion still important to many people?

An English Colony

One Settler's Story

Elizabeth, whose last name we do not know, was only sixteen. She was part of a royal family in Sweden. In the early 1600s, there was trouble in her country and Elizabeth was in danger. She had to leave secretly.

Early settlers usually made their way to America in wooden ships and stayed in rooms called cabins. Elizabeth's friends, who were helping her escape, thought it best for her to go as *freight*, or goods on a ship. They decided to hide Elizabeth in a large wooden barrel. She was fed through a small opening on one side of the barrel. When the ship had been out to sea for three or four days, she came out of the barrel and stayed with the other passengers.

Close to the Jersey Shore, the ship was hit by a violent storm and was wrecked. Elizabeth and some of the others made it to shore, but she became separated from the others. She wandered in the wilderness for days. How she survived no one knows for sure, but the shore had plenty of wild berries. Perhaps she ate them to live.

Her wandering came to an end when she met a hunter by the name of Garrison. He guided her to a small village of European settlers. Garrison and Elizabeth fell in love and were married. The couple settled in the town of Bridgeton and had ten children. It is believed that she had over a thousand *descendants*.

Two New Jerseys

In 1676, New Jersey was divided. One part was owned and controlled by Sir George Carteret. One part was owned by the Quakers, who made Burlington their capital.

When Sir George Carteret died, his land was sold. The new owners made Perth Amboy the capital of East Jersey. Now there were two capitals and two governments for the colony of New Jersey.

William Penn, other Quakers, and a group of people from Scotland purchased East Jersey. Soon an argument started over who really had the right to the land. Who had the right to sell property, collect rent, and receive taxes?

Pirates

One of New Jersey's frequent visitors was Captain William Kidd. Captain Kidd was a famous pirate who lived in New York. Kidd stopped on his way back from looting ships to see his friends who lived on the coast of East Jersey.

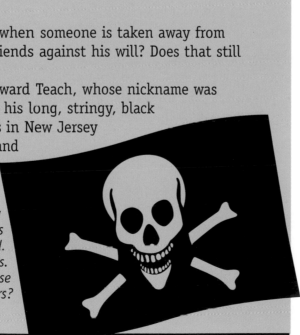

The following news item appeared in *The American Weekly Mercury*:

Perth Amboy, June 2, 1723—
Publick Notice is hereby
given that one John Wilson, Marriner being
on board the sloop William
. . . was taken by Pyrates, the said Wilson was
forced on board the Pyrate Sloop against
his will.

What word do we use when someone is taken away from his home, family, and friends against his will? Does that still happen today?

Another pirate was Edward Teach, whose nickname was "Blackbeard" because of his long, stringy, black beard. His favorite spots in New Jersey were the Delaware Bay and Delaware River areas.

A "Jolly Roger" is a flag with a skull and crossbones or other scary symbol. Pirates flew these flags. What message would these flags send to others?

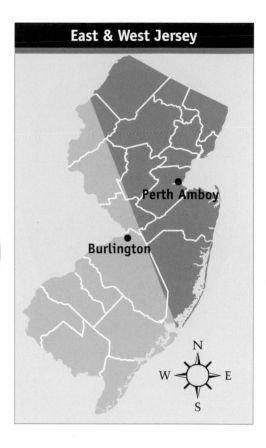

East & West Jersey

Perth Amboy

Burlington

N
W   E
S

People in East Jersey preferred to live in little towns while the people in West Jersey lived on large farms that were far apart.

An English Colony

Queen Anne of England

A Royal Colony

Twenty years after New Jersey was divided, the proprietors gave their right to govern New Jersey to Queen Anne of England. She finally brought the colony together for the first time and named it a *royal* colony. England would control it. Even though New Jersey was a royal colony, the proprietors still had the power to buy and sell land. But they could not rule. The new royal governor lived in New York and governed both colonies.

The Great Awakening

During the 1740s, a religious change happened in the colonies. It was called the Great Awakening. This was a time when many people became very religious. Others changed religions. There was an increase in church membership. People started to become interested in religions other than the Church of England.

French and Indian War

France and Great Britain were *rivals*. Each was trying to win a race. The prize was more colonies and a greater empire. Both countries believed colonies would make them rich and powerful. The colonies' natural resources would be used to make products which could be sold or traded. The people living in the colonies would help build the empire. Countries were ready to go to war over their empires. And they often did.

France and Great Britain fought over colonies in the French and Indian War. It was the final contest to decide who was most powerful in the New World. French soldiers attacked the British forts and villages on the Canadian border. British soldiers attacked the French. Both sides got help from Indian *allies*.

For nine years the two countries fought. The war finally ended when the British captured the French cities of Quebec and Montreal in Canada. A peace treaty was signed. Great Britain got control of Canada and all the land between the Atlantic Ocean and the Mississippi River. Now Great Britain was the most powerful country in the world.

We call it the French and Indian War because the British fought both the French and the Indians.

Barracks

During the war, every colony had to supply places where the soldiers could live. The places were called *barracks*. New Jersey was ordered to set up five barracks, which were located at Trenton, Perth Amboy, Elizabethtown, New Brunswick, and Burlington. The barrack in Trenton is the only one still standing. It is now a museum where people can visit and see how the soldiers lived in the 1700s.

Both the French and the British built forts to defend themselves against attack.

William Franklin Becomes Governor

In the same year the French and Indian War ended, New Jersey named William Franklin, the son of Benjamin Franklin, as governor. He was born in America and at thirty-three was thought to be quite young to be a governor.

No one ever dreamed that William Franklin would be the last royal governor of New Jersey. The time was coming when great changes would be taking place between Great Britain and the thirteen colonies.

William Franklin

Activity

Sailing to America

1. How many levels does this ship have?

2. What countries' flags are flying atop the sails?

3. Can you see the bunks where people are sleeping?

4. On deck, can you find the bell?

5. What kinds of things do you think are stored in the bottom of the ship?

Art by Jon Burton

The New Jersey Adventure

Old Newspapers

1. Did you ever have to go to the "Lost and Found" in your school? Read this item printed on February 9, 1764 in *The Pennsylvania Gazzette*. Notice the interesting word choice and spelling that is used.

> "Found, a Silver Watch, on the Great Road leading from Haddonfield to Glouster, the 21st of January last. The Owner, proving his property, and paying Charges, may have it again, by applying to Benjamin Sykes, living in Chesterfield, Burlington County."

   • What do you think the "Charges" might be?
   • Does Mr. Sykes have a street address? How will the owner locate him?

2. Have you ever gone ice skating? Where did you go? Was it indoors or outdoors? Some of the winters during the colonial times were very, very cold. But, at times there were warm days and the ice and snow begin to melt. Here is a news item that appeared in *The American Weekly Mercury* in 1737. Observe where capital letters are used and the spelling and use of some of the words.

> "The Ice in the River Delaware remains yet and People continue to pass over it but 'tis now becomes so rotten that several Men and Horses have broke through and narrowly escap'd drowning."

   • How do people cross the Delaware River today?

Chapter 4 Review

1. Explain Richard Nicolls's plan to get people to settle in Albania.
2. Who replaced Richard Nicolls as governor of Albania? What was his special announcement to the settlers?
3. Why did many settlers from Scotland, Ireland, and France come to New Jersey?
4. Who were the Quakers, and what special set of rules did they have? Who was their leader?
5. Name the capitals of East and West Jersey.
6. Who united the colony?
7. Why did the people of New Jersey want their own governor? Who was the first governor of New Jersey?
8. What was the main reason for the French and Indian War?
9. Who was the last royal governor in the colony of New Jersey?

Colonial Life

THE TIME
1630–1768

PEOPLE TO KNOW
John Woolman
John Witherspoon

PLACES TO LOCATE
Elizabeth
Perth Amboy
New Brunswick
Trenton
Burlington
Middletown
Mount Holly
Princeton
New York
Philadelphia
Hudson River
Delaware River

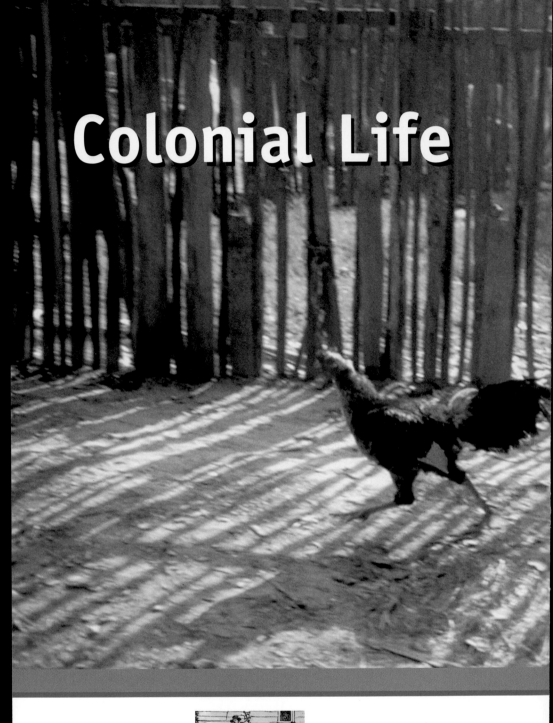

timeline of events

Dutch immigrants come
to New Jersey.
– – **1630s** – –

1676
An iron factory is started
in Shrewsbury.

| 1630 | 1645 | 1660 | 1675 | 169 |

1667
The English take control
of the colony.
Proprietors rule.

chapter 5

(Photo from Colonial Williamsburg)

TERMS TO UNDERSTAND
diversity
flax
hemp
craftworker
apprentice
indentured servant
slave
kinsfolk
game
loom
lye
moral
stocks

1723
Stage wagons are used to move people and goods in the colony.

1754
John Woolman, a Quaker, writes against slavery.

1768
John Witherspoon becomes president of the College of New Jersey.

1705 — 1720 — 1735 — 1750 — 1765 — 1780

1746
The College of New Jersey (Princeton University) is started.

1766
Queen's College (Rutgers University) is started.

A Colonist's Life

AS EARLY AS THE 1700s, NEW JERSEY was a place of great *diversity*. About half of the settlers were English. In some areas people spoke Dutch, German, Swedish, or French more than English. In other places you could hear Scottish, Welsh, or Irish accents. Black slaves from Africa also lived in the colony. The population was growing.

A Growing Colony

Because families had so many children, and because people began to come from other places, New Jersey grew quickly.

At first, most families farmed. They looked for places with good soil near streams. Soon, however, people opened stores and other businesses in towns.

By 1750, New Jersey had six real cities: Newark, Elizabethtown, Perth Amboy, New Brunswick, Trenton, and Burlington. In addition, it had many smaller towns and villages.

Immigrants coming to New Jersey were encouraged to bring dried peas, dried beef, oatmeal, beer, cheese, butter, salt, garden seeds and tools, cloth and clothes, bedding, table utensils, crocks, guns, and gun powder. They also needed money to buy horses, pigs, and chickens once they got here.

Dutch homes were common in New Jersey.

Illustration from North Wind

The first task for new arrivals in New Jersey was to clear the land and build a home.

Making a Home

The first thing a family did was build a small log cabin. They looked for trees that were about the same size around, chopped them down, stripped them of their branches, and stacked them to make the walls. Then they added a roof. Sometimes they just dug a cave in the side of a hill until they could build something better. The people also had to cut their own wood for a barn and fence.

As soon as they could, people began to build permanent houses. Many homes were made of stone. It took a lot of work to gather stones and carry them to where a house was being built. Because it was so hard, the two-story stone houses were usually quite small at first. As the family and farm grew, more rooms were added onto the house. Colonial stone houses were so sturdy that many of them are still around today.

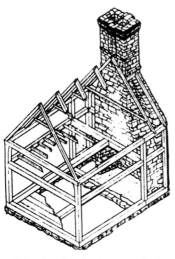

This simple design made it possible for the early settlers to put up stone homes.

Colonial Life

▲ Photo by Susan Myers

The settlers learned to grow corn from the Indians.

Working for a Living
Farming

People in the colony had different ways of earning a living. Most of the people were farmers. They grew crops such as wheat, barley, rye, *flax*, *hemp*, oats, beans, Indian corn, peas, tobacco, onions, melons, apples, pears, peaches, and "all sorts of green trash in the Summer time," as one Middletown settler put it. They also raised cattle, pigs, oxen, and horses. They sold their crops and animals for money.

Farming was very hard work. Before a farmer could plant seeds, he had to clear the land of trees, brush, and rocks. To get the soil ready for planting, he had to guide a plow pulled by horses or oxen.

Farmers needed tools, seeds, and animal feed to do their job. Where would they get these goods? Most of the time they bought them from merchants. Merchants are people who sell goods to make money. Merchants sold their goods to farmers and to other colonists.

"German farmers take very good care of their farms. . . . They deny themselves everything costly [so] they soon become rich."

—Theophile Cazenove, a traveling writer

Craftworkers

There were also *craftworkers* in the colony. They were shoemakers, tailors, candlemakers, glassblowers, or coopers (barrel makers). Settlers who knew a skill, such as weaving or tanning leather, were soon able to buy their own land.

Young men sometimes found work as *apprentices.* An apprentice was a young person who lived with a craftworker and learned the trade. The master provided food, clothes, and a place to live. Some apprentices started as young as seven years old and worked until they were twenty-one.

This woman is making candles. Candles gave light to read and sew by in the evening.

Indentured Servants

Indentured servants were people who found someone already living in the colony to pay for their trip to America. In return, they had to work on that person's farm or in his home for five to seven years. Indentured servants worked very hard for many years. They got food and a place to sleep, but they didn't get paid.

Slaves

Some people came to the colony as *slaves*. Slaves were taken from their homes and forced to work in a new place. Most slaves were black people brought from Africa. They did not get paid for their work and they had no freedom. They were bought and sold to work on farms and in homes.

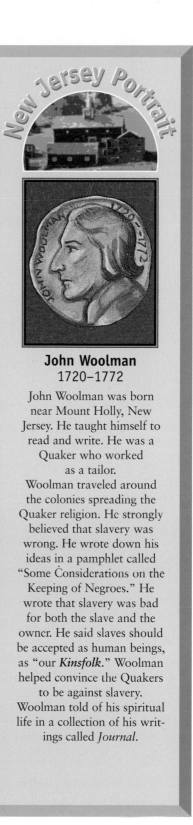

New Jersey Portrait

John Woolman
1720–1772

John Woolman was born near Mount Holly, New Jersey. He taught himself to read and write. He was a Quaker who worked as a tailor.

Woolman traveled around the colonies spreading the Quaker religion. He strongly believed that slavery was wrong. He wrote down his ideas in a pamphlet called "Some Considerations on the Keeping of Negroes." He wrote that slavery was bad for both the slave and the owner. He said slaves should be accepted as human beings, as "our *Kinsfolk.*" Woolman helped convince the Quakers to be against slavery. Woolman told of his spiritual life in a collection of his writings called *Journal.*

Jobs in Colonial New Jersey

Look at the list of jobs below. Are any of the jobs still around today? If so, which jobs are done by both men and women today? Which job would you have wanted if you were a colonist?

Apothecary (pharmacist)

Attorney at Law

Baker

Barber

Blacksmith

Boatman

Brewer (makes beer)

Bricklayer

Brickmaker

Butcher

Carpenter

Chairmaker

Clergyman (works for the church)

Clerk

Clockmaker

Clothier (makes or sells clothes)

Collier (coal miner)

Cooper (makes barrels)

Cutler (makes or sells knives)

Feltmaker (makes felt for hats)

Gentleman (owns and manages property)

Glazier (sells glass for windows)

Glover (makes or sells gloves)

Hatter (makes or sells hats)

Innkeeper

Ironmaster

Laborer

Mariner (ship captain)

Mason (builds with stones or bricks)

Merchant (buys and sells goods)

Miller (owns or operates a mill)

Millwright (builds the machines for a mill)

Nurseryman (sells plants)

Pedlar (sells door-to-door or in the streets)

Perukemaker (makes wigs)

Physician

Plasterer

Ropemaker

Saddler

Sawyer (saws logs or boards)

Schoolmaster

Secretary of Province

Shallopman (boat man)

Shipwright (makes wooden ships)

Shoemaker

Silversmith

Surveyor (measures the land)

Tailor

Tanner (tans leather)

Tinsmith

Treasurer (manages money)

Weaver

Wheelwright (makes wheels and carriages)

Whaleman (goes out to sea to hunt whales)

Woolcomber (prepares wool for use)

Sharing the Work

Men, women, and even children worked hard to make the colony a better place. They were turning the wilderness into towns and settled farms. They were learning to govern themselves and to build churches and schools.

Men at Work

The men on the farm spent their days outside doing hard, back-breaking work. Fields had to be cleared of trees and stumps so that gardens could be grown and livestock put out to pasture. The cut trees were then dragged to the sawmill and cut into boards for building barns, houses, furniture, and fence rails. The treetops were cut for firewood, and stumps and roots were used to make fences for the animals until better fences could be built.

The men also had to plow the cleared fields with wooden plows pulled by oxen or horses. Then, with the help of their children, they planted, weeded, and tended their crops.

Just like the American Indians, many pioneer families relied on wild *game* as a source of meat. The men spent much of the time hunting deer, wild turkeys, and other game.

Women at Work

The women were in charge of the household chores. They worked hard from before the sun came up to after it went down at night. There were plenty of people to feed and care for, including babies. Making food to feed a large family took many hours each day.

During the winter, the cooking was done in the cabin fireplace. In the summer, the women did their cooking and baking outside so the cabin wouldn't get too hot.

Besides meat, milk, and eggs, families ate mostly what they grew. They made stews with vegetables and wild game. They baked bread and corncakes. They used fresh fruits to make pies and other desserts. Maple syrup tapped or drained from trees and honey from beehives were used when they wanted to make something sweet.

Cows gave milk, which the people drank and used to make butter and cheese. When the settlers butchered a cow for beef, they also made rope from its tail and leather from its hide.

In a colonial kitchen, women cooked over the fire and dried other food items by hanging them from the ceiling.

Making clothes was another job that took up a woman's time. Each family member needed a summer work outfit, a winter work outfit, and a Sunday church outfit. Using a spinning wheel and a *loom*, the women turned sheep's wool and flax into cloth. If the family could afford it, a tailor came to the house and sewed the cloth into underwear, shirts, bed sheets, tablecloths, and aprons. However, most people made their own clothes.

Every fall, the women made soap for washing clothes. All year long, they saved the ashes from the fireplace. Then they put the ashes into big barrels and added water. The gooey liquid that seeped out at the bottom was called *lye*. The women put the lye in a big kettle over the fire and added animal fat. When the liquid cooled, it hardened into lye soap. It was a dirty job, but it made the clothes clean.

Marriage

People married at a young age. Sometimes a bride was only fourteen years old. Young married couples did not have to worry about being poor as long as they were willing to work. There was plenty of land and food at a good price.

Most colonists had many children. Children were very important because they helped do the work on the farm and in the home.

Colonial families had fun celebrating events such as a birth or marriage. Getting together, singing, eating, and dancing helped them forget the hard work on the farm.

Everyone gathered around the fireplace for light and heat. Notice how large the fireplace is.

What do you think?

Why do you think people got married so young in colonial times? Why do you think people today have fewer children?

Children at Work and Play

There was so much work to be done that children as young as four were given chores. They weeded the fields, carried wood for the fire, took out the ashes, and fed the animals. By age thirteen, children could do almost as much work as an adult.

For fun, children played with dolls made from cornhusks and balls made of wood. They played card games, ran races, and sang songs.

If you were a young boy in the colony, you helped your father on the farm or worked as an apprentice. If you were a young girl you helped your mother use a large iron pot to cook over the fire and looked after the babies and younger children.

What do you think?

"Children are the poor man's wealth."
—Danish proverb

What do you think this saying means? Do you think it applies to children in colonial times? Why?

Colonial children would see how far and fast they could roll a hoop. Try it yourself with a Hula-Hoop.

Early Schools

At first, the settlers learned at home and at church. Villages were far apart, so children who did not study at home received little schooling.

If there was a school, it was run by the family's church. It taught religion and *morals* as well as reading and writing. The Bible was often the only book used in school. The school was one room, where all the grades were taught together.

The schools shut down in the summer, when the children were needed for outdoor work on the farm. Wealthy families sometimes hired private tutors for their children. However, this was rare.

Even though early schools were not fancy, education was very important to the people. In fact, for a while New Jersey was the only colony with two colleges. The College of New Jersey (now Princeton University) was started in Elizabeth by a group of Presbyterians. Later the college was moved to Newark, and then to the town of Princeton.

Queen's College (now Rutgers University) was started by men from the Dutch Reformed Church. Like many colleges of the time, its purpose was to educate men who wanted to become ministers.

Children learned their ABCs from the Bible and a hornbook, like this one. Paper was very expensive. In order to protect it from getting ripped, the horn of a cow, bull, or ox was cut very thin. The page was then sandwiched between two sheets of this thin, clear horn. To make sure it didn't slip out, a wooden frame was placed around it.

Belief in God was very important to most people in the colonies. Read the lesson on the page of the hornbook. Where do you think the lesson came from?

Rutgers University

• Princeton University

Linking the past and the present

Only men went to college then. Now men and women are supposed to have the same educational opportunities. Are there any ways in which girls and boys are treated differently in the school system today?

What do you think?

Some people today like the idea of the one-room schoolhouse. They say learning is easier when the older children can help the younger ones. Do you think school would be better with mixed grades? Or do you think it would be harder to learn that way?

Rivers and Roads

The people depended on the land and water around them. They used the many streams and rivers for travel and transportation. They used them to water farmlands and pastures. Streams and rivers provided power to run sawmills and gristmills (where grain is turned into flour). Bays and harbors were sometimes used for shipping, but the rocky shores were dangerous places for boats. Rivers were a safer way to ship goods.

New Jersey's first roads followed old Indian trails. Early roads were often in need of repair. New roads had to be built and old ones had to be rebuilt to connect the colonial capitals of Perth Amboy and Burlington. Also, New Jersey was the major pathway between New York and Philadelphia. Soon, small companies were competing to offer transportation from city to city.

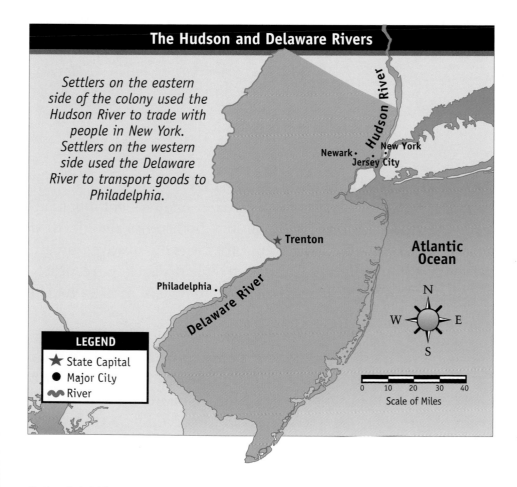

The Hudson and Delaware Rivers

Settlers on the eastern side of the colony used the Hudson River to trade with people in New York. Settlers on the western side used the Delaware River to transport goods to Philadelphia.

Hudson River

Newark • • New York
Jersey City

★ Trenton

Philadelphia •

Delaware River

Atlantic Ocean

N
W E
S

0 10 20 30 40
Scale of Miles

LEGEND
★ State Capital
● Major City
〰 River

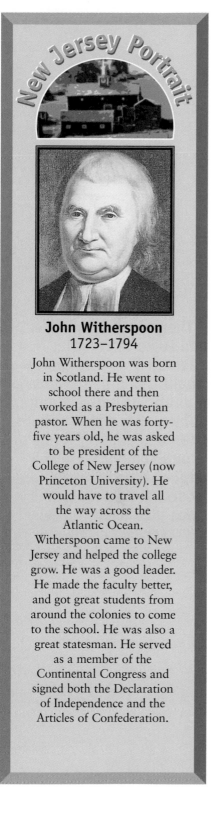

John Witherspoon
1723–1794

John Witherspoon was born in Scotland. He went to school there and then worked as a Presbyterian pastor. When he was forty-five years old, he was asked to be president of the College of New Jersey (now Princeton University). He would have to travel all the way across the Atlantic Ocean. Witherspoon came to New Jersey and helped the college grow. He was a good leader. He made the faculty better, and got great students from around the colonies to come to the school. He was also a great statesman. He served as a member of the Continental Congress and signed both the Declaration of Independence and the Articles of Confederation.

Taverns and Inns

Taverns and inns began to dot the main roads. Most taverns had bedrooms where weary travelers could rest. Taverns were also important to the townspeople. They had large public rooms for meetings, balls, elections, and celebrations. Local people went to the tavern to relax, meet neighbors, gossip, and talk politics.

Taverns were important places to early settlers.

There were strict laws and rules in colonial New Jersey. If a person was caught using bad language in public or being drunk in public, that was a serious offense. Common forms of punishment were the *stocks* and the whipping posts. The death penalty was also used for more serious crimes.

Diseases and Folk Medicines

Diseases often troubled the colonists. They had brought folk medicine with them from the old country. Sometimes they learned new remedies from the Indians. But that was not always enough. In 1642 the English and Swedes at Salem Creek were nearly wiped out from an unfamiliar disease. In Salem, measles hit. In Burlington, people died from smallpox and yellow fever.

There were no hospitals with modern equipment. It was not unusual for a mother and father to have more than half of their babies die. Many children died from diseases before their fifth birthday. Not many people lived to be more than sixty-five years old. In fact, the average person lived only to the age of thirty-five or forty.

The New Jersey Adventure

Population of the New Jersey Colony

1. How many different years are shown on the graph?
2. Did the number of people in the colony rise or fall?
3. How many more people lived in New Jersey in 1700 than in 1680?

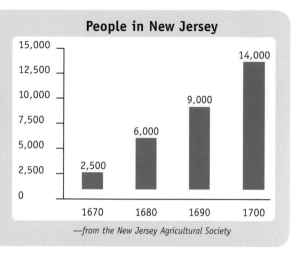

People in New Jersey

—from the New Jersey Agricultural Society

Chapter 5 Review

1. What is an indentured servant? How is an indentured servant different from a slave?
2. What was the most popular job in the colony?
3. List three crops that farmers grew.
4. What kind of work did the men and boys do?
5. What kind of work did the women and girls do?
6. What were the first two colleges in New Jersey?
7. What university did John Witherspoon help start?
8. How did the people use rivers?
9. What were taverns used for?
10. Why did so many children die very young?

Geography Tie-In

1. List New Jersey's major rivers.
2. Explain how rivers helped colonists and goods reach villages in many different parts of New Jersey.
3. Describe how rivers linked New Jersey to the other colonies.

THE TIME
1764–1783

PEOPLE TO KNOW
Samuel Baldwin
John Adams
Paul Revere
King George III
George Washington
Patience Lovell Wright
William Livingston
Molly Pitcher
Lord Cornwallis

PLACES TO LOCATE
Newark
Great Britain
Boston, Massachusetts
Delaware River
Greenwich
Philadelphia,
   Pennsylvania
Lexington,
   Massachusetts
Concord, Massachusetts
Trenton
Morristown
Springfield
New York City
Yorktown, Virginia

1765
Britain passes the Stamp Act,
requiring an official stamp
on legal documents.

1770
All taxes are dropped
except the tea tax.
The Boston Massacre

timeline of events   **1760**   **1763**   **1766**   **1769**

1764
Britain passes the Sugar Act
to pay for war.

1767
Britain passes the Townshend
Acts, taxing glass, tea, paper,
paint, etc.

chapter 6

Crossroads of the American Revolution

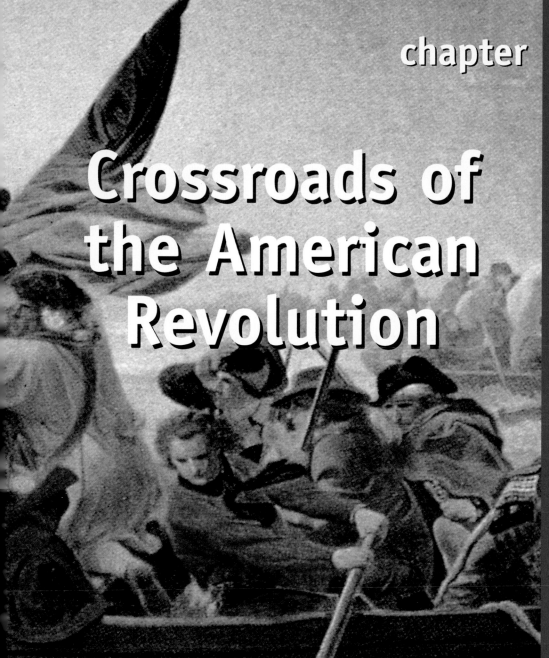

Washington crossing the Delaware River (Painting from North Wind)

TERMS TO UNDERSTAND
revolution
deed
compromise
evict
riot
rebellion
customs house
delegate
militiamen
Loyalist
Patriot
mercenary
fleet

1775
The Battle of Lexington and Concord starts the American War for Independence.

1776
The Second Continental Congress meets to declare independence. The Declaration of Independence is signed by the delegates.

1781
British troops surrender to General George Washington and his army after the Battle of Yorktown.

| 1772 | 1775 | 1778 | 1781 | 1784 | 1787 |

1774
Delegates to the First Continental Congress meet in Philadelphia.

1775–1783
American War for Independence

Early Signs of Trouble

HAVE YOU EVER BEEN OUTSIDE when suddenly the sky became darker and soon, before you knew it, the sound of thunder was in your ears? That's just the way the American Revolution started in the thirteen colonies.

A *revolution* is when one government takes over another government.

The towns of Caldwell, West Caldwell, Verona, Essex Fells, Roseland, Cedar Grove, North Caldwell, Caldwell Township, and Livingston were once the Horseneck area.

The Horseneck Riots

Over one hundred years before the American Revolution, a group of settlers started the Newark colony. The colony was located in a part of New Jersey called Horseneck. The Indians had sold the land to the settlers in exchange for gunpowder, lead, axes, coats, blankets, and other supplies.

A few years later, the settlers bought some more land from other American Indians in the area. Both groups signed an agreement called a *deed*. According to British law, settlers were not allowed to make deeds with Indians. But the law was not easy to understand. Many of the settlers went ahead and made deeds with Indians anyway.

Some British men had already been given land by the British government. They thought they still owned the land. They tried to *compromise* with the settlers so each group could have part of the land, but the settlers refused. Finally, the men became angry and started *evicting* the settlers from the land.

Samuel Baldwin, a settler, was arrested for cutting down trees. He was held in the Newark prison. Some of the settlers set him free, and on the way back to Horseneck, they started *riots*. The newspapers called the riots a *rebellion* against Great Britain. The riots kept on happening and some of the settlers were taken to court. Some had to give back land to the British men and some had to pay fines. Bad feelings against Britain started to grow.

Acts that Added Wood to the Fire

The people in the colonies were not very happy in the 1760s. Britain needed money. The country was looking for ways to pay for past wars it had fought in Europe and America.

Britain passed the Sugar Act, which placed a tax on all sugar and molasses sold in the colonies. Next, the Stamp Act was passed. The Stamp Act said a stamp was needed on all papers such as marriage and birth certificates. Colonists had to pay for the stamp. This made them angry. Most of them would not pay the tax. The Stamp Act failed, so Britain got rid of it.

Another set of taxes, called the Townshend Acts, taxed glass, tea, paper, paint, and other things most people needed. The colonists would not buy the things from Britain or pay this tax either. By 1770, only one of the taxes remained—the tea tax.

The Sons of Liberty were a secret group of men who were against Great Britain's taxes. John Adams, Samuel Adams, and Paul Revere were all members.

John Adams

Linking the past and the present

A tax is money the government charges on goods and property. Taxes pay for services such as education, public health services, and highway repair. Do we pay taxes today? What is taxed?

Words Turn into Action

One morning, a group of boys and men began throwing snowballs at a British soldier who was standing guard at a *customs house* that collected taxes in Boston, Massachusetts. The guard got nervous and called some soldiers to help him. The crowd got bigger and a riot soon broke out. People in the crowd started throwing snowballs and hitting the soldiers. One of the soldiers accidentally fired his gun. Soon the soldiers started firing at everyone. Five men were killed, and eight more were wounded. This event is known today as the Boston Massacre.

Ten British soldiers were put on trial. Some lawyers worked to get them free. One of the lawyers was a future president of the United States, John Adams. Two soldiers went to prison.

What do you think?

John Adams belonged to the Sons of Liberty. Why do you think he volunteered to be the lawyer for the British soldiers? If you were a lawyer, would you have defended the British? Why or why not?

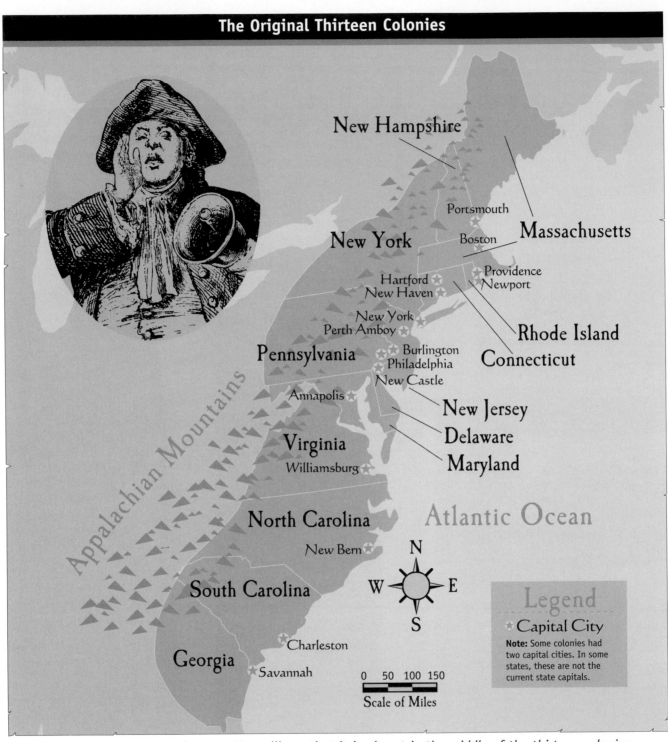

The Original Thirteen Colonies

New Hampshire

Portsmouth

New York

Boston

Massachusetts

Providence
Newport

Hartford
New Haven

Rhode Island

New York
Perth Amboy

Connecticut

Pennsylvania

Burlington
Philadelphia
New Castle

Appalachian Mountains

New Jersey

Annapolis

Delaware

Virginia

Maryland

Williamsburg

North Carolina

Atlantic Ocean

New Bern

N
W   E
S

South Carolina

Legend

★ Capital City

Note: Some colonies had two capital cities. In some states, these are not the current state capitals.

Charleston

Georgia   Savannah

0   50 100 150

Scale of Miles

Locate New Jersey on the map. You will see that it is almost in the middle of the thirteen colonies. New Jersey's geography made it the one colony that both sides wanted to control. New York and Philadelphia, two very important cities, could be reached very easily because there were no mountains to cross. Both armies moved back and forth across the state so much that very soon people were calling New Jersey the "Pathway of the Revolution." Almost one hundred battles were fought on Jersey soil.

The Boston Tea Party

The colonists were so angry about the taxes that they decided to teach Britain a lesson. Three British ships full of tea arrived in Boston Harbor. A group of colonists dressed up like Indians and raided the ships. They put the captain and crew below deck and dumped all of the tea overboard. This was called the Boston Tea Party.

New Jersey's Tea Party

The Boston Tea Party did not stop Britain from trying to ship tea to the American colonies. The colonists spotted a ship carrying tea near the shore of the Delaware River. The ship secretly sailed up the Cohansey River and unloaded its cargo of tea in Greenwich, New Jersey. Members of the Sons of Liberty dressed up like Indians and burned the tea in the center of town. New Jersey had its own "Tea Party."

Greenwich • Cohansey River

Crossroads of the American Revolution

The First Continental Congress

The colonists decided to start working as a team. Riots were happening everywhere. People were not paying taxes. Some felt that no one was speaking up for them in Parliament. (Parliament is the lawmaking group in Britain.) In 1774, the First Continental Congress met in Philadelphia, Pennsylvania. Every colony except Georgia sent **delegates** to the meeting. They were men who would help make the rules. New Jersey sent five delegates to the meeting.

Soldiers left their wives and children to fight for independence.

Revolution Begins

British soldiers marched towards Lexington, Massachusetts. Their goal was to locate and destroy everything that might be used to start a war against them. They looked for guns, powder, lead to make bullets, small cannons, and anything else that the colonists might be hiding. Three Sons of Liberty—Paul Revere, William Dawes, and Samuel Prescott—rode all night to warn the people that the British soldiers were coming. The next morning, about seventy colonial **militiamen** (soldiers) were face to face with the British soldiers.

The British soldiers ordered the militiamen to clear the way. There was shouting on both sides. Suddenly a shot rang out. Who fired it? Neither side said it was responsible. Then more shots were fired. When the smoke cleared, eight Americans were killed and ten were wounded.

That first shot is known as the "shot heard 'round the world." It has become a symbol for the American Revolution. The British moved on and finally searched the buildings in Lexington and Concord. The battle marked the beginning of the American War of Independence.

The War for Independence is also called the Revolutionary War. Look up the word "revolutionary" in the dictionary. Explain why the war was given that name. What does "independence" mean?

Colonists and British soldiers fought at Concord Bridge.

Paul Revere's Ride

An American poet, Henry Wadsworth Longfellow, wrote a poem called "Paul Revere's Ride." It begins like this:

> *Listen, my children, and you shall hear*
> *Of the midnight ride of Paul Revere*
> *On the eighteenth of April, in Seventy-five;*
> *Hardly a man is now alive*
> *Who remembers that famous day and year.*

The Declaration of Independence

Thomas Jefferson

Do you think that all colonists were angry with Great Britain? If you said "No," you are correct. A large group stayed loyal to the king. They were known as *Loyalists*. Those who wanted independence were called *Patriots*. Every colony had both groups. Many families were split between the two. Fathers against sons, mothers against daughters, brothers against brothers—on and on it went.

The Continental Congress had to meet a second time. Twelve out of the thirteen colonies voted for independence. New York did not vote.

Thomas Jefferson was asked to write a letter to King George and Parliament. The letter said that because they had been treated unfairly, the American colonies were cutting off all ties with Great Britain. On July 4, 1776, the letter was approved.

In August, delegates from all thirteen colonies signed the letter. This letter is known as the Declaration of Independence. The colonies were now on their way to becoming independent states, but it was not going to be easy.

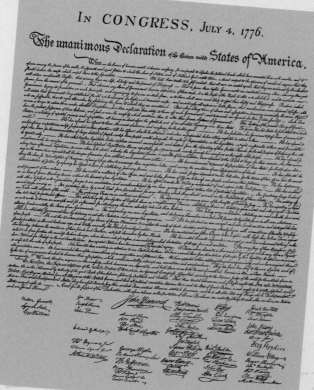

John Hancock, a delegate from Massachusetts, went up to the table and said something like this, "I'm going to sign my name so that King George will be able to read it without using his spectacles!" He wrote very large. Even today, when anyone signs something very important, we say that the person is signing his "John Hancock."

What do you think?

How do you think British King George III reacted when he read the Declaration of Independence?

The New Jersey Battlefield

The Battle of Trenton

Soon after the war started, the British hired some German soldiers to fight for them. When a soldier is paid to fight for another country, he is called a *mercenary.* These mercenaries, also called Hessians, had fought many battles. A group of them was stationed in Trenton.

On Christmas night, 1776, during a heavy snowstorm, George Washington and his men crossed the Delaware River a few miles north of Trenton. It took about nine hours for all the American soldiers to cross the river in rowboats. When the soldiers were all across, the cold march southward to Trenton began.

The Hessians were warned several times to keep an eye out for the Americans, but they didn't pay any attention to the report for two reasons. First, they were celebrating Christmas with plenty of eating, playing cards, and drinking. Second, the weather was so bad that they thought that no one would dare to cross the Delaware. It was filled with large chunks of floating ice.

The storm didn't stop the Americans. Before anyone knew what was happening, the buildings at Trenton were in the hands of George Washington and the Continental Army. The battle lasted less than an hour. The Hessian officer was killed, along with about 500 of his men. The Americans lost only two men.

No one expected the Americans to do what they did at the Battle of Trenton. The British were shocked. After Trenton, the Americans had hope that the British Army could be beaten. Independence could become more than a dream.

The Battle of Monmouth

The British Army began marching across New Jersey towards New York City. Right behind them were Washington and his army. The British soldiers were very tired, not only from the march, but also from carrying their fifty-pound backpacks. General Washington felt that the Americans had a great chance to win

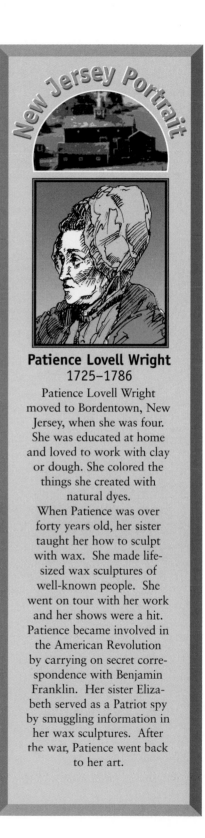

New Jersey Portrait

Patience Lovell Wright
1725–1786

Patience Lovell Wright moved to Bordentown, New Jersey, when she was four. She was educated at home and loved to work with clay or dough. She colored the things she created with natural dyes.

When Patience was over forty years old, her sister taught her how to sculpt with wax. She made life-sized wax sculptures of well-known people. She went on tour with her work and her shows were a hit. Patience became involved in the American Revolution by carrying on secret correspondence with Benjamin Franklin. Her sister Elizabeth served as a Patriot spy by smuggling information in her wax sculptures. After the war, Patience went back to her art.

this battle because his men were now well trained. Washington's army stopped the advance of the British, who boarded ships back to New York. The British Army did not win any important battles in New Jersey after that day.

Molly Pitcher

In the days of the revolution, many wives went with their husbands to battle. They cooked and took care of their husbands if they became wounded. Mary Hays, whose nickname was Molly, was one of those brave women who was by her husband John's side. His job was to help load and fire a cannon. During the battle, Molly carried water in a large wooden bucket to the American troops. The soldiers would call out, "Molly, the pitcher!" Soon they were just saying, "Molly! Pitcher!"

When a British bullet wounded John, Molly dropped the pitcher and took his place at the cannon. Later, George Washington heard of her courage and thanked her in person. She is now known as Molly Pitcher.

Mary Hays became known as Molly Pitcher.

New Jersey Portrait

William Livingston
1723–1790

William Livingston was born in New York and educated at Yale University. He became a lawyer and moved to New Jersey. He lived near Elizabethtown on an estate named Liberty Hall.

He served as governor of New Jersey and general of the New Jersey Militia. Livingston was a delegate to the Continental Congress and one of the signers of the United States Constitution. He said, "Whoever draws his sword against his prince must fling away the scabbard [sheath for a sword]." What do you think this means? Who is "his prince"?

The New Jersey Adventure

The Ford Mansion in Morristown was General George Washington's winter headquarters. How many chimneys can you find? Why would this house need more than one?

George Washington

This is the room George Washington and his officers used to make plans for the year. How many quill (feather) pens can you find? Where do you think the feathers came from?

Washington's Winter Headquarters

A young widow, Mrs. Ford, offered her home to George Washington for his winter headquarters. Besides Mrs. Ford and her four children, Martha and George Washington and about fifteen officers lived in the home.

Spring came, and along with it came some good news. A young French general, Lafayette, arrived at the Ford Mansion and told General Washington that France was sending soldiers to help the Americans.

Inside view of a soldier's hut. Why aren't there any closets? How would a person know what things belonged to him?

Soldiers' huts were built at Jockey Hollow. Can you tell the season of the year this picture was taken? Why do you think the huts were built on a hill?

Soldiers in Winter

American soldiers were setting up their camp about five miles away at a place called Jockey Hollow near Morristown. They built cabins in which twelve soldiers could live. To get logs for the cabins, thousands of trees had to be cut down, trimmed of their branches, and cut to the right size.

Snowstorms and strong winds made life very hard for everyone. The worst storm in over one hundred years occurred during this winter. Not all the soldiers had cabins. Some lived in tents. Food was running out and many of the soldiers became sick. Some soldiers died.

A very patriotic woman, Rhoda Farrand, her two daughters Hannah and Bet, and many other women who lived in the Morristown area knitted thousands of pairs of socks for the American troops. As Rhoda sat on the back of a wagon knitting the socks, she called out to everyone to help Washington's army. Her son Dan drove the wagon from town to town and from farm to farm.

Tempe Wick

During the Revolution, some soldiers spent the winter at the Wick family farm. One day, Mr. Wick's daughter, Tempe, was riding her horse near the farm. Some soldiers stopped her and said they wanted the horse for Washington's army. Instead of giving them the horse, Tempe quickly galloped away.

As soon as she reached her house, Tempe walked her horse through the kitchen and into her bedroom. When the soldiers reached the farm, they checked the barn, the outhouses, the fields, and even the woods near the farm. They could not find Tempe or her horse.

Some say that the horse was hidden for up to three weeks in Tempe's bedroom. When the troops were gone, out came the horse. Tempe and her horse were seen galloping around the farm again.

The Battle of Springfield

On June 23, 1780, the British began to march towards Morristown. Just a few days before, at the Battle of Connecticut Farms, there had been an accidental shooting and death of a local woman. The Americans got so angry that they pushed the British all the way back to Elizabethtown. The British were met by the Americans at the town of Springfield. After a short but hard fight, a few hundred militiamen turned back the British soldiers. The British never reached Morristown.

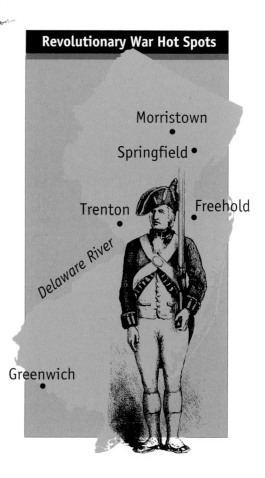

Revolutionary War Hot Spots

Morristown

Springfield

Trenton

Freehold

Delaware River

Greenwich

Victory

With the help of the French, the war was finally brought to an end. Over 5,000 soldiers and a great *fleet* of ships arrived from France. The French also lent the Americans money to buy food, clothing, weapons, and even to pay the soldiers.

Washington and the French generals planned to attack the British in the Chesapeake Bay area. However, while they were doing this, British General Lord Cornwallis moved his troops to the York River. As he did this, the French fleet blocked the entrance to the York River. They cut off any chance of Cornwallis receiving help from British ships carrying soldiers and supplies.

Cornwallis was trapped. He surrendered to General Washington. The Revolutionary War was over. A peace treaty was signed in 1783.

Over 17,000 men from New Jersey fought in the Revolutionary War.

Flag Symbols

Early American flags had many symbols. A symbol is something that stands for something else. The thirteen stars and thirteen stripes in the early flag stood for the thirteen colonies. The thirteen stars forming a circle stood for the unity of the colonies.

Design your own flag. Add your own symbols. What symbols stand for important things you are proud of? Draw or paint your flag on a piece of paper.

Chapter 6 Review

1. Why did the settlers riot at Horseneck?

2. Name the three acts that were very unpopular in the thirteen colonies.

3. Who was responsible for dumping British tea in Boston Harbor and burning tea in Greenwich, New Jersey?

4. Why did the British march on the towns of Lexington and Concord?

5. Why was Christmas a good time to attack the Hessians at their barracks in Trenton?

6. Explain the difference between a Loyalist and a Patriot.

7. Explain why New Jersey is called the "Pathway of the Revolution."

8. Why was the Battle of Yorktown very important to the Americans?

THE TIME
1776–1804

PEOPLE TO KNOW
William Livingston
William Paterson
Phyllis Wheatley
George Washington
Alexander Hamilton
Aaron Burr

PLACES TO LOCATE
Rhode Island
Philadelphia, Pennsylvania
Virginia
Connecticut
Princeton
Trenton
Washington, D.C.
New York
Newark
Weehawken

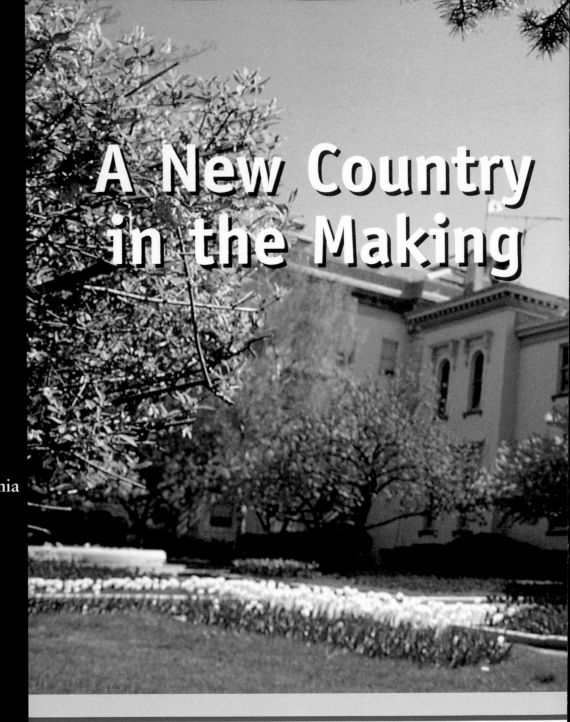

A New Country in the Making

timeline of events

1776
New Jersey drafts a constitution.
William Livingston becomes
New Jersey's first governor.

1787
The United States Constitution is written.
New Jersey becomes the third state to ratify the
U.S. Constitution. New Jersey becomes a state.

1775   1780   1785

1783
Princeton is the nation's capital.

1783–1785
Trenton is the nation's capital.

TERMS TO UNDERSTAND
descent
excerpt
representative
debate
ratify
legislature
exclude
barter
currency
interpret
federal
local
bill
majority
veto
treason

Our state capitol building is in Trenton. (Photo by Walter Choroszewski)

1790
The Constitution is ratified
by all thirteen states.

1791
The Bill of Rights is added to
the Constitution.

1804
Aaron Burr kills Alexander
Hamilton in a duel.

| 1790 | 1795 | 1800 | 1805 |

1790
Trenton is chosen as
New Jersey's capital.

1792
First state capitol building is completed.
Governor William Paterson publishes
the first state laws.

Who is standing, talking to the Constitutional Convention? These men were important heroes who wrote our Constitution. They are often called the Founding Fathers.

John Adams said the United States has "a government of laws and not of men." What did he mean by that?

ONCE AMERICANS WERE FREE of Great Britain's control, the country needed a set of laws to live by. Except for the state of Rhode Island, men from all of the twelve other states met in Philadelphia at the Constitutional Convention. They did not want a king, a queen, or a president to have all of the power. They wanted a way to rule themselves.

In writing the Constitution, the men gave the government of the United States of America only certain powers. Power was also given to the states. That way the people in one state could make laws for themselves that might be different from the laws in another state. The people thought this kind of government was best.

The New Jersey Adventure

The Bill of Rights

A Bill of Rights was added to the Constitution later. It listed rights that no government could take away from the people. Some of the rights were the right to belong to any religion, to speak freely, and to write and print whatever they thought was important. These were rights that were not allowed in many other countries.

What do you think?

Why did the people think it was very important to add the Bill of Rights to their new Constitution? Are the rights important to you?

Phillis Wheatley

Phillis Wheatley was the first poet of African descent in all of North America. She was one of the very few slaves at this time who had some type of education. In 1775, she wrote a poem for George Washington. Here is part of that letter and poem:

Sir,
   I have taken the freedom to address your Excellency in the enclosed poem:

Proceed, great chief, with virtue
   on thy side,
Thy ev'ry action let the goddess
   guide.
A crown, a mansion, and a
   throne that shine,
With gold unfading, Washington!
   be thine.

Read Phillis Wheatley's words carefully. What do you think the phrase "gold unfading" means?

The goddess in the poem was Columbia. Phillis Wheatley came up with the word and the idea of Columbia as a symbol of the new United States. The capital of our country is called Washington, D.C. The D.C. stands for the District of Columbia.

The parchment paper has yellowed and faded but the words of the Constitution are still the basis for our government today. Two hundred years after it was written, President Ronald Reagan said, "Our Constitution is being celebrated not for being old, but for being young." What did he mean?

Government for the People

Part of government is the rules people work out for living together. Your school may have a student government. Large countries and small groups all have governments. Different countries in the world have different governments.

The United States is run by *representatives*. Instead of all the people voting for the laws, people elect representatives to vote for them. The people still have the power and the final authority. If the representatives don't vote the way the people want them to, the people can vote for someone else next time.

At the Constitutional Convention, there were *debates* about how representatives should be chosen.

The Virginia Plan

Virginia was one of the largest states. The delegates from Virginia suggested that the number of representatives in Congress should be based on how many people lived there. This was known as the Virginia Plan.

The New Jersey Plan

Delegates from New Jersey suggested that each state should have the same number of representatives. These delegates wanted smaller states like Delaware, Rhode Island, and Connecticut to have the same amount of representatives as larger states. This was known as the New Jersey Plan.

Connecticut Compromise

The Connecticut Compromise called for both plans to be used. It set up two houses, or groups, of Congress. One group, called the Senate, would have two representatives from each state no matter what the population was. The second group, called the House of Representatives, would be made up of representatives according to a state's population. Larger states would have more representatives than smaller states.

Approximately 700,000 slaves were living in America at that time. Most of them lived in the South. There were about 10,000 slaves in New Jersey. The delegates agreed that the states would count each slave as three/fifths of a person in the population count for representatives. This meant that five slaves would equal three white men.

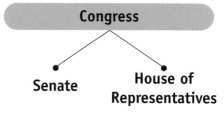

Today, New Jersey sends two senators and thirteen members of the House of Representatives to Washington, D.C., to help make our laws.

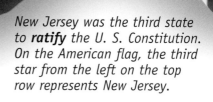

*New Jersey was the third state to **ratify** the U. S. Constitution. On the American flag, the third star from the left on the top row represents New Jersey.*

A New Country in the Making

New Jersey became a state on December 18, 1787.

What do you think?

Representatives from New Jersey and all of the fifty states go to Washington to make laws for the whole country. What problems might there be with so many people from so many places trying to make laws for everyone?

Selecting a National Capital

At different times, the two towns of Princeton and Trenton were our young nation's capital. Some people thought that Trenton should be our nation's capital because New Jersey was almost in the middle of the thirteen states. That was not to be. The District of Columbia was created outside of Alexandria, Virginia. Washington, D. C. does not belong to any one state. It belongs to all fifty states. It is the capital of the United States of America.

Selecting a State Capital

Do you remember reading about the "two New Jerseys" with one capital in Perth Amboy and the other in Burlington? New Jersey adopted a constitution on July 2, 1776, two days before the signing of the Declaration of Independence. The time had come for the state to select one city to be its capital. Trenton was selected because it was near the center of the state.

Capital Cities Today

Government representatives meet and make laws in the capital city.

- The capital of the United States is Washington, D.C.
- The capital of New Jersey is Trenton.

People who live in New Jersey have to follow the rules of both the United States and the New Jersey governments.

It all adds up: New Jersey
+ 49 other states
+ Washington, D.C.
= TEAMWORK!

Our State Constitution

When New Jersey's constitution was written in 1776, a new *legislature* was created to make up the laws. The legislature had two parts. One part was the Assembly and the other was the Senate. The people of New Jersey elected their representatives to the legislature. They also elected a governor.

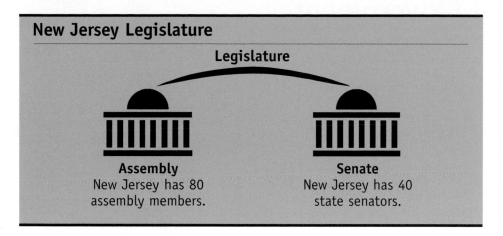

New Jersey Legislature

Legislature

Assembly
New Jersey has 80 assembly members.

Senate
New Jersey has 40 state senators.

Who Can Vote?

In the first constitution, the right to vote was given to all property owners. Both men and women could vote. About thirty years later, the legislature voted that African Americans and women no longer could vote. They were *excluded* from this privilege.

New Jersey's constitution has been changed many times. The constitution we use today was approved in 1947. Anyone who is a citizen of the United States and is eighteen years old can vote.

What do you think?

Do you think that eighteen-year-olds are responsible enough to vote for government leaders? Why or why not?

Rights for All

Our state constitution, like our federal constitution, gives all of us certain rights. The government cannot take away these rights. What are some of our important rights?

- Enjoying and defending life and liberty
- Acquiring and owning property
- Obtaining safety and happiness
- Electing government leaders
- Worshiping God, but not being forced to pay for any church
- Speaking and writing freely
- Getting a fair trial
- Not being put into jail for debt

Whose Currency Is It, Anyway?

Most of the people in the colonies were farmers. When they needed something, they **bartered** for it with their neighbors. But, paper money was being used more and more each day.

Each state was allowed to have its own **currency**. It could be paper or coins. There was a big problem with that, especially if you lived in one state and went to buy something in another state. People from Connecticut were having a problem using their money in New Jersey. New Jersey's money was not being accepted in New York. It was getting worse every day.

Each state also taxed anything from another state that was sold in their state. Before anyone knew it, the states were arguing. Instead of thinking like one nation, they were beginning to act like separate little countries.

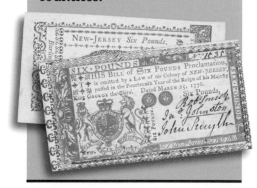

Three Branches of Government

Both the state and federal government have three branches. They are the legislative, executive, and judicial branches. Branches of government each have special jobs. This is called a "balance of power."

Legislative Branch

The men and women elected to make up our state laws are called legislators. They belong to either the state Assembly or the Senate. They make the laws.

On the legislative branch, find the politicians who are debating and giving speeches.

Executive Branch

The executive branch carries out the laws. The governor is the head of the executive branch and is elected by the people of New Jersey. The governor can serve for a four-year term but cannot serve for more than two terms in a row. The governor's duties are to see that the laws are obeyed, be commander in chief of the state's militia, and call meetings of the legislature whenever he or she thinks it is necessary.

Find the governor answering questions from people. Find a reporter typing up the conference.

Political Parties

Political parties are groups of people who share the same ideas about government. Most people choose either the Democratic Party or the Republican Party. Those are the two main parties in New Jersey and in the rest of the United States. There are also other parties, called third parties. As another choice, some citizens do not belong to any party. They run for office or vote as Independents.

Find the political parties on the tree trunk. Which parties do the elephant and donkey represent?

Judicial Branch

The courts make up the judicial branch of the government. The judicial branch *interprets* the laws. Laws are made to protect the rights of everyone. Sometimes these laws are broken. The rights of the citizens have to be protected. The people breaking the laws are punished. The courts try to settle arguments between people in a peaceful way.

The most powerful court in the state is the Supreme Court. A judge called a chief justice and six other justices make up the court. The governor chooses these seven justices. However, the Senate must approve the choices.

Find the judge, jury, and court reporter.

Art by Jon Burton

Levels of Government

Federal Government

In the United States, there are three **levels of government—** *federal*, state, and *local*. Each level has the three branches of government (executive, legislative, judicial).

Level	Place	Head of Executive Branch
Federal	United States	President
State	New Jersey	Governor
Local	County, City, Town, Village	Mayor

Our federal, or national, government can do certain things that the state government cannot do. The state government can do certain things that the federal government cannot do. This was promised when the delegates wrote the Constitution.

The federal government can control trade with other countries, set up a postal system, and print money to be used in every state and throughout the world. It organizes the army, air force, navy, marines, and coast guard. It also builds and repairs highways.

There are many other things our federal government can do. However, it cannot treat one state better than the others. It cannot give anyone a title like king or queen. It cannot keep anyone from having a fair trial.

On the opposite page, find the capitol building and other government buildings. At the bottom of the page, find a war tank. In the corner there are flags and soldiers marching. This is to show that our country's defense is part of the federal government.

New Jersey's Representatives

How do the people of New Jersey help make the laws of the federal government? By sending representatives to the United States House of Representatives and Senate. Along with representatives from all of the other states, they vote on laws for the whole country.

114

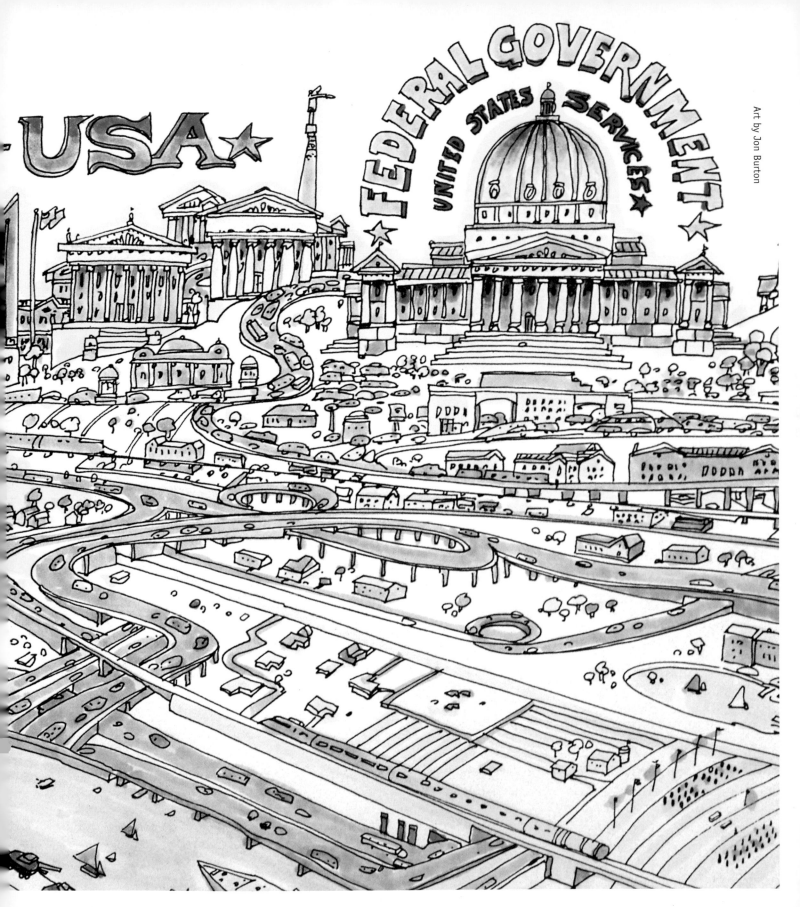

Art by Jon Burton

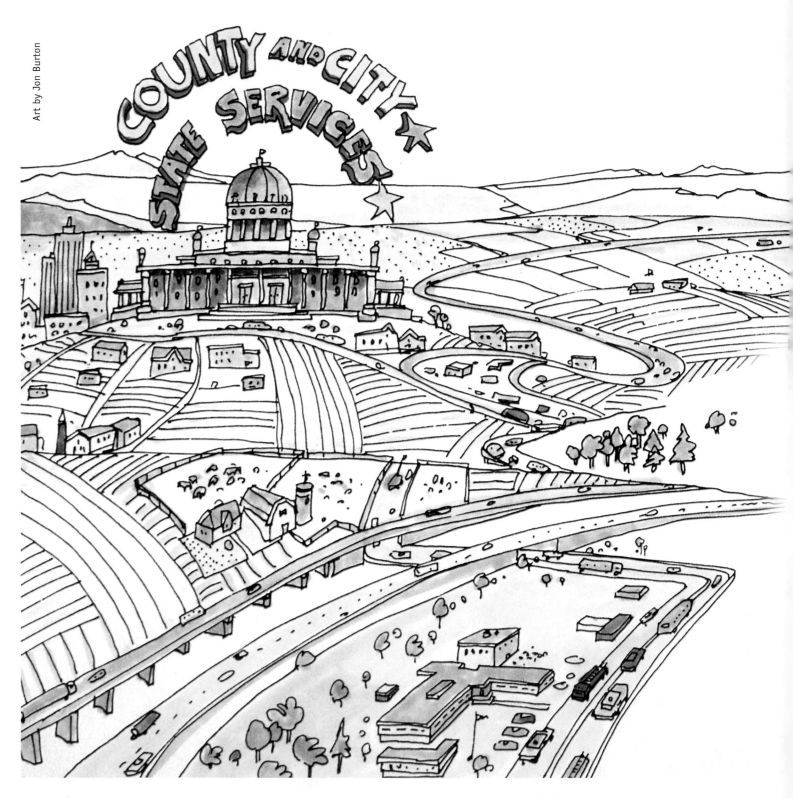

County and City State Services

State Government

Here are some of the things a state government may and may not do. A state can make the laws for the safety and health of its citizens. It can have a say as to how elections are run. It can control what goes on in the schools and how the governments of every town and city are set up. Some of the things it cannot do are try to tell the federal government what to do, or refuse to send delegates to Washington, D.C. A state cannot print its own currency.

On the opposite page, find the school. Schools are state services.

County Government

New Jersey is divided into twenty-one counties. Each county has a town that is the county seat. There is usually a courthouse there, where the courts are located. Births, deaths, and marriages are recorded at the courthouse. If your family owns property, a map of the property is recorded in your county courthouse.

Officials known as freeholders govern in the counties. The term "freeholder" is from colonial times, when only property owners could hold office. They were known as freeholders.

Find the county courthouse. Find the fire truck. It is provided by the county.

City Government

Another kind of local government even closer to home is city government. There are different kinds of city governments. Cities are usually run by a mayor or a city manager, with a city council. Larger cities have larger governments than small towns. Cities make rules about what kinds of buildings can be built in different regions of the city. They often keep houses separate from businesses. They make sure schools are in safe places. They make laws about speed limits in the city.

On the opposite page, follow the streets. They are controlled by the city.

Counties and County Seats

A New Country in the Making

Taxes Pay for Services

New Jersey's constitution gives our state, counties, and cities the power to collect taxes. Tax money helps pay for services all of the people can use. Taxes come in many forms. People and businesses pay taxes on the money they make. Each county collects taxes on land, homes, and buildings. These are called property taxes.

What is tax money used for? Taxes pay for making and fixing local streets. They pay for plowing snow. Taxes pay for libraries where you can check out books. Cities use tax money to pay for clean water. They have garbage picked up. If you play soccer on a city team or swim in a city pool, you are using a city service. Cities also pay for parks where you can play ball and have picnics.

Taxes pay for public education. If you go to a public school, your building, your books, and your teachers are paid with tax money. If you go to a private school, your parents pay for most of these things.

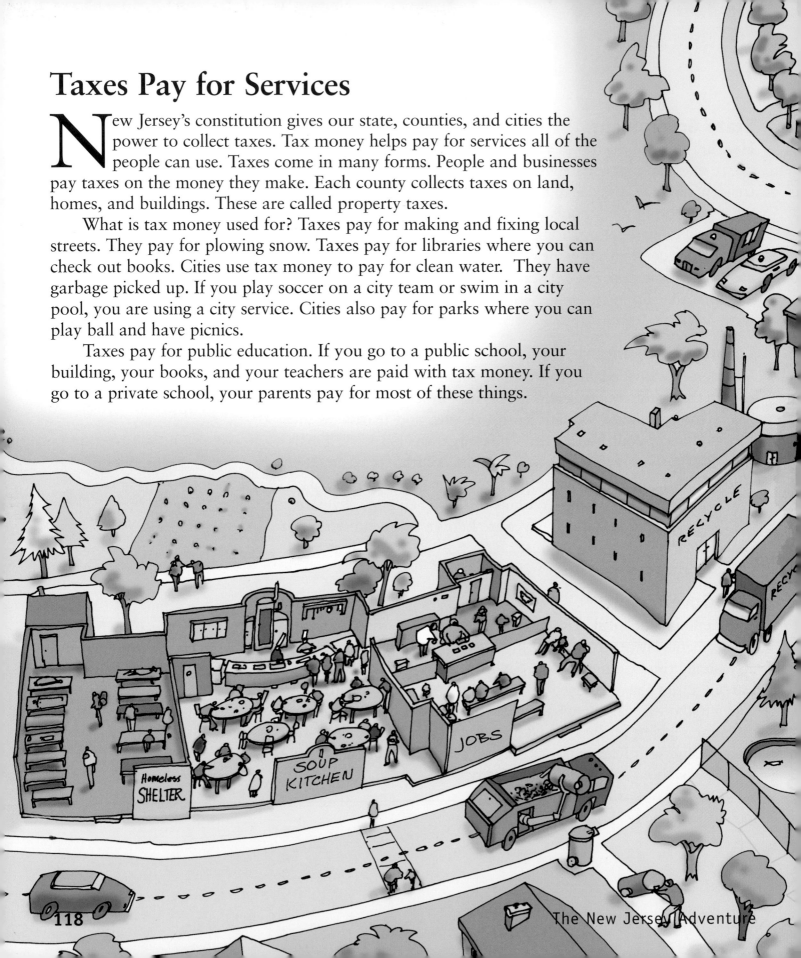

RECYCLE

JOBS

SOUP KITCHEN

Homeless SHELTER

RECY

The New Jersey Adventure

Some public services are provided by volunteers. In New Jersey, many of our fire fighters and rescue workers are volunteers. How many public services can you find in this town?

Making a Law

The legislature meets each year to decide which *bills* become new laws. A bill is a written idea for a new law. The bill is sent to either the Senate or the Assembly. After legislators debate about the good and bad points of a bill, a vote is taken. If a *majority* votes "yes" on a bill, it goes to the other group. If a majority of that group also votes "yes," it goes to the governor. If a majority of representatives votes "no" on the bill, it goes no further. It does not become law.

If the governor believes the bill would make a good law, he or she signs it and it becomes a new law for New Jersey. If the governor does not believe the bill would make a good law, it is sent back to where it started. This is called a *veto*.

After a veto, the legislators can vote again if they wish. If two-thirds of the Senate and two-thirds of the Assembly vote for the bill, it can become a law without going to the governor again. This is one way the power of making laws is shared by both branches of government. It is an important part of our constitution.

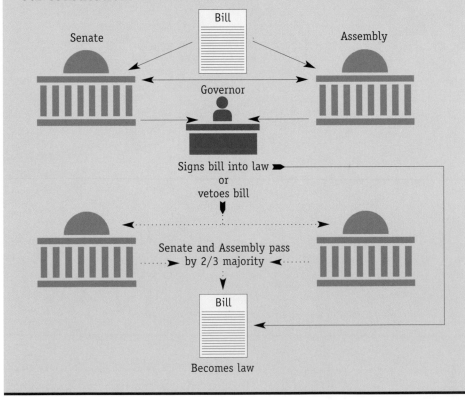

The New Jersey Adventure

It's Against the Law!

Our government is responsible for making laws. Some very strange ones still exist in New Jersey. No one enforces them, but they are on the records. Here are two funny laws:

Your mother has told you not to slurp your soup. But if you do it in a public restaurant in New Jersey, you could be arrested. It's against the law!

If you are in Newark, don't ever try to buy ice cream after 6 p.m.—unless, of course, you have written permission from your doctor. Otherwise, it's against the law!

Taking Part in Government

Citizens have a right and a duty to take part in their government. Only the citizens can make a representative democracy work. What can adults do? What can you do?

- Vote.
- Run for office.
- Tell your representatives and council members what you want them to do (by letter, fax, e-mail, telephone, or in person).
- Write letters to the editor of newspapers to tell other people how you feel.
- Get the facts (from newspapers, magazines, TV, and radio reports).
- Learn about the candidates running for office (from leaflets, newspapers, speeches, TV, and radio).
- Take part in meetings, marches, and protests.
- Give speeches.

Alexander Hamilton and Aaron Burr

Alexander Hamilton went to school at Elizabethtown. He was one of the founding fathers and the secretary of the treasury. He believed in a strong federal government, including electing a president for life.

Aaron Burr was born in Newark and attended Princeton University. He worked as a lawyer before becoming vice president when Thomas Jefferson was president of the United States.

Hamilton had a long-standing disagreement with Burr. As was the custom at that time, Hamilton and Burr agreed to settle their dispute in a duel. One hot summer day, the two met in Weehawken. Burr shot Hamilton, who died the next day.

Today, killing someone who disagrees with you is against the law. How could these two men have solved their problems peacefully?

Alexander Hamilton

Aaron Burr

Aaron Burr killed Alexander Hamilton in a duel.

The New Jersey Adventure

You Be the Judge!

A judge is a very important person. He or she must listen carefully to both sides before deciding what to do. The judge can fine people, send people to jail, or just tell them about being good citizens. In each case, a judge uses the laws that were written by the legislators to help decide what to do.

Now it is your turn to be the judge. Read the story. Then write how you would have the boys settle their problem.

Jason rides his shiny new black and silver bike to school. He carefully locks it up. After school, his friend Matthew asks to borrow the bike for a while. Jason agrees and tells Matthew to take good care of it and to bring it back before dark.

Matthew enjoys riding the bike and stays out late. When he gets home it is dark and his family is calling him in for the night. Matthew lays the bike down on the ground and goes in. In the morning, the bike is gone. It has been stolen.

Jason is very upset about his new bike. He thinks Matthew and his family should buy him a new one. Matthew says his family doesn't have enough money to buy a new bike. He says it was too dark to return the bike the night before. He says he had planned to go back outside later and put the bike in a safe place, but he forgot. He says it was not his fault the bike was stolen.

Chapter 7 Review

1. Explain what the Americans needed after they were free from British rule.
2. Explain the difference between the New Jersey Plan and the Virginia Plan.
3. How did the Connecticut Compromise finally bring peace to the Constitutional Convention?
4. Why was Trenton chosen to be New Jersey's capital?
5. Did everyone have the right to vote according to New Jersey's first and second constitutions? Explain your answer.
6. Which branch of government has the responsibility to make the laws?
7. Which branch of government interprets the laws?
8. Which branch of government enforces the laws?
9. What are some city and county services?

THE TIME
1787–1846

PEOPLE TO KNOW
Alexander Hamilton
William Paterson
John Fitch
Samuel Morse
Alfred Vail
John Stevens

PLACES TO LOCATE
England
Paterson
Passaic River
Millville
Indian Mills
Millstone River
Hoboken
Morristown
Jersey City
Phillipsburg
Hudson River
Delaware River
Raritan River
Newark
Trenton

timeline of events

1787
John Fitch demonstrates
the first steamboat on
the Delaware River.

1805
The first ship drydock is
built in Jersey City.

1785

1795

1805

1792
Paterson, the first
planned industrial city,
is founded.

1806
The first bridge is built across
the Delaware River at Trenton.

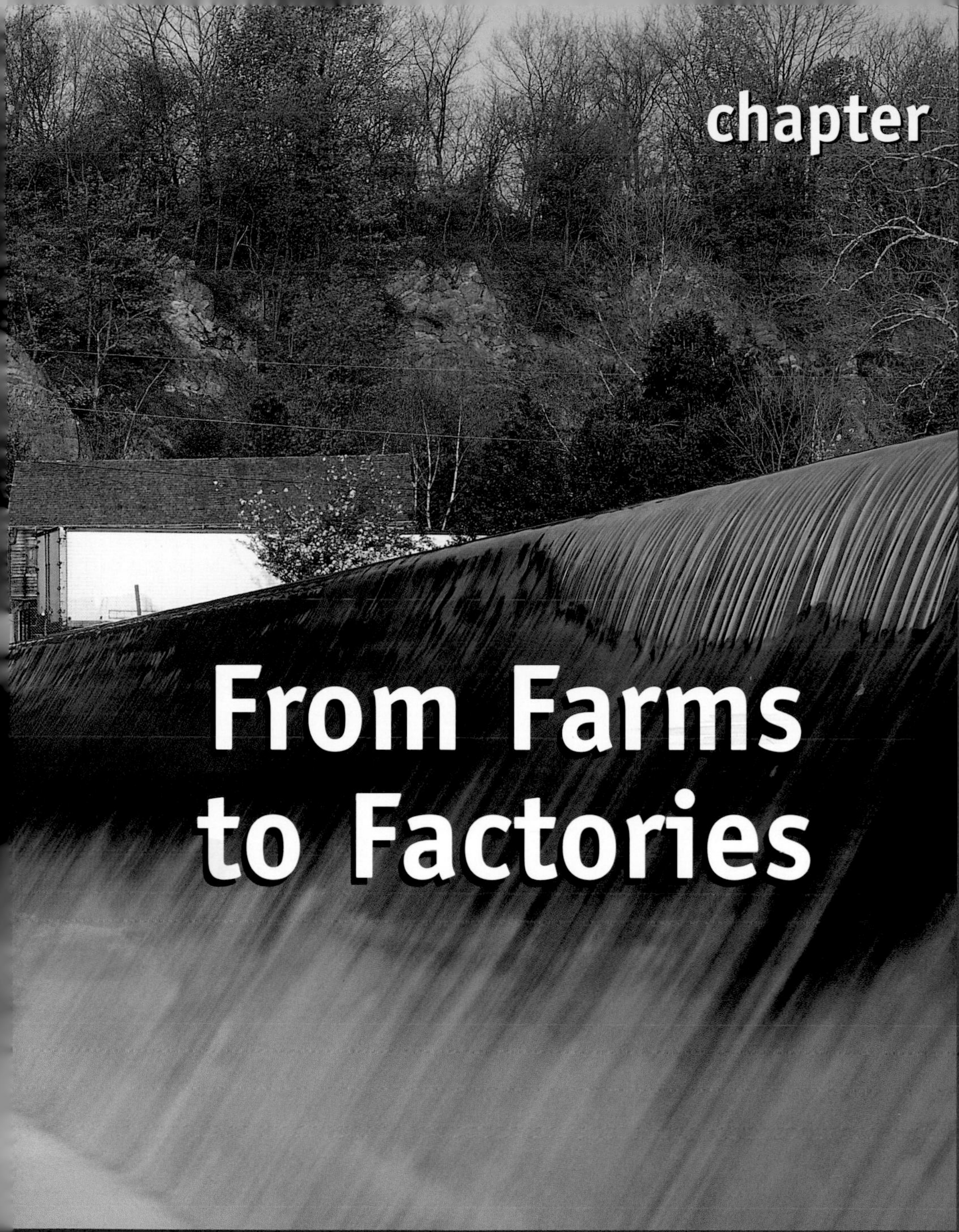

Chapter 8

From Farms to Factories

TERMS TO UNDERSTAND
raw materials
manufacture
economy
committee
raceway
canal
textile
wage
theory
transmit
barge
towpath
inclined plane
lock
locomotive
express train

Clinton Mill is on the Raritan River. (Photo by Tom Till)

1811 A steam ferry runs between Hoboken and New York.

1812–1815 War of 1812

1815

1824 John Stevens of Hoboken demonstrates the first steam engine.

1825

1831 The Morris Canal opens.

1833 The Camden and Amboy Railroad is started.

1834 The Delaware and Raritan Canal opens.

1835

1837 The first locomotive is built in Paterson.

1838 Samuel Morse and Alfred Vail develop the magnetic telegraph.

1845

1846 The world's first official baseball game is played at Hoboken.

The Second Revolution

BEFORE THE AMERICAN REVOLUTION, *raw materials* were shipped over to England. There they were *manufactured* into tools, clothes, and household items. Then the items were shipped back and sold to the colonists. After the United States became independent of Great Britain, the colonists had to manufacture many of the things themselves.

In Europe, machines were invented that could make things faster than people could make them by hand. This was called the Industrial Revolution. The Industrial Revolution was a shift from an *economy* based on agriculture, or farming, to one based on manufacturing and industry.

The Industrial Revolution changed the way people worked. Before, people grew their own food and bought only the few other things that were necessary. After, people made things to be sold. People started to buy more things instead of making items themselves.

Paterson, An Industrial City

Alexander Hamilton (who helped write the Constitution) and other Americans believed that it was necessary for the United States to be on its own when it came to manufacturing. The Society for Establishing Useful Manufacturers (SUM) was founded by Hamilton and others. They decided that a manufacturing city should be started. People would manufacture different things the people needed, especially textiles. A place located at the Great Falls of the Passaic River was chosen. The Passaic River had a good supply of waterpower that would turn the waterwheels in the mills.

The SUM *committee* called the city Paterson in honor of Governor William Paterson. Water from the river above the falls would be directed to the town using hand-dug *raceways* or *canals*. A cotton mill and fifty homes were built for the workers and their families. Plans were also made to build a sawmill so lumber could be cut to build homes and factories.

War of 1812

The War of 1812 was a conflict between the United States and Great Britain over water and shipping rights. Because of the war, the supply of **textiles** from Great Britain was cut off. Colonists had to make things themselves. Mills opened in Paterson to meet this demand.

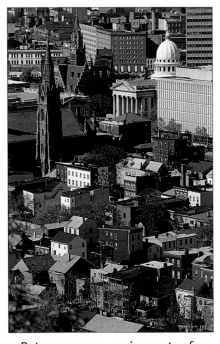

Paterson was a major center for silk factories, machine shops, and railroad locomotives. Paterson is still a leader in textiles in the United States.

Soon the number of factories increased in Paterson and all throughout the state. Where there were factories, large cities began to grow. Men and women were soon leaving the farms to work for higher *wages*.

Can you see why the rushing water of Great Falls at Paterson has so much power? Great Falls is the second highest falls on the East Coast.

Linking the past and the present

During the Industrial Revolution, Americans began making many of their products in factories. Where are most of the products you use made? Check the labels of your clothes, games, and other common items to see where they were manufactured.

From Farms to Factories

Textiles are fabrics and cloth made from knitting or weaving.

Manufacturing textiles was a major industry in New Jersey.

A cotton mill has machines that weave thread into cloth. The machines are powered by water.

Mills

Wheat was a very important crop in the country. Sometimes farmers grew more than they needed and shipped the rest down the river to merchants. The merchants bought the wheat and had it ground into flour.

Millers, the people who owned and ran the mills, were very important to a town. Many towns offered land and even money to get a miller and his family to move to their community. Some even went as far as building the mill for him.

If there were no rivers or fast-moving streams near the town, large ponds were dug to hold water. The water was directed to the mill's waterwheel by digging a deep ditch that led to it.

In the late 1700s, a mill near Philadelphia started to use a new way to bring grain into the mill. Before, men at the mill had to carry the heavy sacks of wheat up to the bin that fed it into the millstone. The millstone ground the grain into flour.

The new way used a long chain of large buckets that were filled with the grain at the ground level. The buckets were moved by waterpower up to the large open bin above the millstone. There a worker dumped the grain into the bin as the millstone turned. The flour from the millstone poured onto a wide moving belt and into a large bag. Then the flour bags were lowered to the ground.

What do you think?

Do you think it took more or less workers to mill the wheat using the buckets? What might happen to the price of flour?

Activity

Mill Names

There are places in New Jersey that were named because a mill was located in or near the town. A few examples are Millville, Indian Mills, and Millstone River.

Work with a friend on a map of New Jersey and see how many places with "mill" in the name you can locate.

▲ Photo from North Wind

Waterwheel

Water from a river or waterfall makes a waterwheel go round and round. As the waterwheel turns, it generates power. Its power turns a millstone, which can grind wheat into flour. The flour was packed in sacks and loaded on to wagons. Sometimes the flour was packed in wooden barrels. The wagons took the flour to private customers and to markets. That's how the mills made money.

From Farms to Factories

The long oars on the John Fitch *were moved by a steam-powered engine.*

On the Move

After New Jersey workers produced goods, the goods had to be transported to New York or Philadelphia to be sold in markets. New methods were needed to move the goods. One answer was the invention of the steamboat.

An inventor by the name of John Fitch thought that it might be possible for a steam engine to move a boat. He worked very hard to prove that his **theory** could work. Fitch developed the first American steamboat. He ran a steamship service that carried people and goods from Philadelphia to different towns in New Jersey.

Later, John Stevens's company was operating a steamboat service from Hoboken to Philadelphia. His boat, named the *Phoenix*, traveled along the New Jersey Shore on its way to Philadelphia. This was a first for steamboat travel because no other steamboat had ever traveled on the Atlantic Ocean.

A Message Through a Wire

Samuel Morse and Alfred Vail developed the telegraph near Morristown. The telegraph was an important way of sending news across the country because there were no telephones. A message such as "The war is over!" got to people long before a letter could be sent by train.

A telegraph machine could *transmit* messages over an electric wire. Men cut down thick tree trunks, put the ends into the ground, and then strung up wires on the tall poles from city to city.

Messages were tapped into the telegraph machine by using a system of dots and dashes called the Morse code. An operator touched a key quickly for a dot and held it down longer for a dash.

Morse Code

A • —	S • • •
B — • • •	T —
C — • — •	U • • —
D — • •	V • • • —
E •	W • — —
F • • — •	X — • • —
G — — •	Y — • — —
H • • • •	Z — — • •
I • •	1 • — — — —
J • — — —	2 • • — — —
K — • —	3 • • • — —
L • — • •	4 • • • • —
M — —	5 • • • • •
N — •	6 — • • • •
O — — —	7 — — • • •
P • — — •	8 — — — • •
Q — — • —	9 — — — — •
R • — •	0 — — — — —

Figure out this famous Morse code signal: • • • — — — • • •

What do you think?

The first telegraph message was: "A patient waiter is no loser." What do you think this means? How does it relate to the telegraph? Does the message relate to your life?

Canals

If someone had to ship only a few things that were not too heavy, a wagon or a steamboat would do just fine. But factories were growing. People had to find a way to move heavy things like coal and iron across the state.

Some states were using canals, or wide ditches filled with water, to move goods. Now it was New Jersey's turn to dig them. Water from nearby rivers and lakes was used to fill the ditches. Some of the canals had boats with steam engines on them. Many of them had flat-bottom boats, or *barges,* that were pulled by horses or mules. The animals walked along a road called a *towpath* and were led by someone who guided them along their way.

Horses or mules often pulled the boats on the canals.

The boat was put on a carriage with wheels. Then it was pulled up with ropes.

Morris Canal

There were two important canal systems in New Jersey. The first was the Morris Canal. It covered almost one hundred miles, from Jersey City on the east to Phillipsburg on the west, from the Hudson River to the Delaware River. A journey on the Morris Canal took about five days. Only parts of the Morris Canal still exist today.

There was a challenge facing canal builders. The land rises over 900 feet from the Hudson River to the Delaware River. An *inclined plane* was used to solve the problem. It was like a large playground slide with tracks on it. As a boat came up to the plane, it was pulled onto a small carriage and then pulled up the plane with the use of ropes. The Morris Canal had twenty-three of these inclined planes. The longest one was over five football fields long.

Delaware and Raritan Canal

The second canal system was called the Delaware and Raritan, or the D&R. The Delaware and Raritan Canal, connecting the Delaware and Raritan Rivers, created an all-water route from New York City to Philadelphia. Barges could make the trip in less than one day as compared to five days on the Morris Canal.

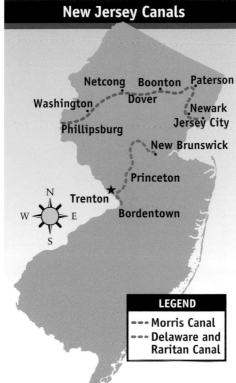

New Jersey Canals

LEGEND
- - - Morris Canal
- - - Delaware and Raritan Canal

How Does a Canal Lock Work?

To make the trip between New Jersey cities, a boat often had to pass through *locks*.

Locks raise or lower boats along their journey. Locks were needed because the water level in one place is higher than the level at another place.

A lock is a space big enough to hold a canal boat, with huge doors on each end. (1) When a boat needs to be lowered, a door opens and the boat enters the lock. (2) Then the door closes behind it. Water is let out of the lock through the door in front of the boat. (3) The water lowers and the boat is lowered. Water keeps running out of the lock until the levels inside and outside are the same. (4) The boat can now float out of the lock and continue its trip.

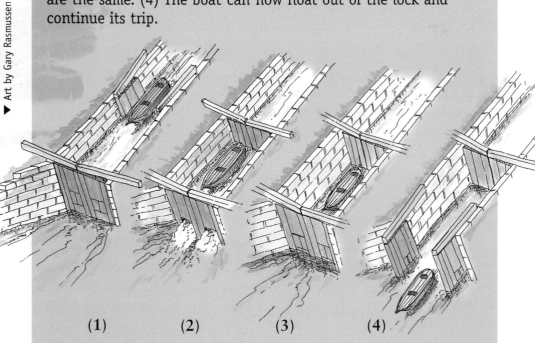

(1)   (2)   (3)   (4)

▶ Art by Gary Rasmussen

On the early trains, people slept, ate, and cooked wherever they could.

Railroads

Early train cars had open sides. There was a danger of sparks from the smokestack burning holes in the passengers' clothing. Later, closed cars were used. Instead of wood, the engines burned coal that made far fewer sparks.

Transportation in New Jersey improved quickly in a short period of time. Even with all the improvements, there was still a need to move people and goods faster. Colonel John Stevens invented the "Steam Waggon." It could go twelve miles per hour. It ran on a circular track next to Stevens's home in Hoboken. A runner could easily beat it in a race.

At that time, some people did not believe that railroads were necessary. They felt they were too expensive. Stevens sent his son Robert to England, where he had a *locomotive* built. The locomotive was named the "John Bull" and it weighed ten tons. It was much too heavy to run on the wooden tracks that were used then. Robert invented an iron track that was held onto the wooden ties with a special iron spike. His inventions are still used on today's railroads.

The first railroad line in New Jersey was the Camden and Amboy Line which opened in 1833. With the new iron tracks, the John Bull could run on the railroad. A person could travel from Philadelphia to New York in seven hours. A steamboat line was available at either end. So, once a person got off the train, he or she could take the steamboat to another city or town.

In time, people began to use the railroad more and more. Many more miles of track were built. At one time, there were over twenty railroad companies in New Jersey. Soon people began to see more trains and fewer steamboats, wagons, stagecoaches, and canals.

Linking the past and the present

New Jersey still has more miles of railroad track than any other state in our country. Today you can take an *express train* from Newark to Trenton in about thirty-five minutes.

As our country grew, so did the steam locomotive.

John Stevens
1749–1838

John Stevens was born in New York City, but lived much of his life in New Jersey. He was one of the first people to use steam power.

First, he developed a steamship that he ran on the Delaware River. The ship was the first steamship to travel in the Atlantic Ocean. Second, Stevens ran a steam ferry from Hoboken to New York City. Finally, he formed the Camden and Amboy Railroad and Transportation Company and made the first locomotive.

From Farms to Factories

Strike One!

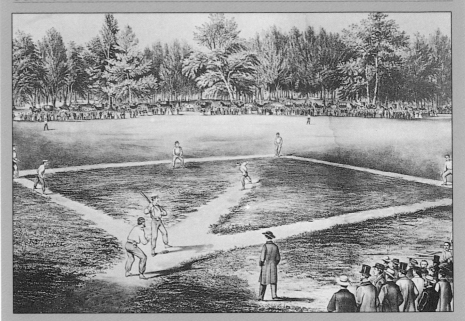

Anybody want to play "Rounders"? In the 1600s, children in England played a game where the players hit a ball with a bat and then ran around bases. There were no written rules at that time, but it was similar to baseball.

Much later, a club was started called the New York Knickerbockers. The players loved the game so much that they wrote down a set of rules. Some of those rules are still used today—the number of people on the field, the number of feet between bases, three outs for each team during each inning, and three strikes for each batter every time he is at bat. There was no such thing as a walk. The batter could stay at bat until he hit the ball or struck out. A strikeout meant that the batter missed hitting the ball three times.

The first official baseball game with rules was played in Hoboken on June 19, 1846, between the New York Knickerbockers and the New York Baseball Club. The final score was:

New York Baseball Club	23
New York Knickerbockers	1

Inventions Make Life Easier

During the Industrial Revolution, many inventions improved people's lives. Machines did hard jobs much faster than people could do them.

Suppose you were an inventor. What invention could you make that would save people from doing a difficult job? Can you think of an invention that might make your life easier? Someone else's life easier? Draw a picture of your invention. Write about what the invention would do and how it could help people.

Chapter 8 Review

1. How did the Industrial Revolution change the way colonists made and sold goods?
2. Why was the city of Paterson started?
3. Where did the power come from to run the mills in Paterson?
4. What did John Fitch invent?
5. How does a boat get from one water level to another on a canal?
6. How did John Stevens change transportation even after he invented the steamboat?

Geography Tie-In

1. How do you think the railroad changed the animal and plant life in New Jersey? How did it change life for people?
2. As a class, talk about the geography theme called "movement." Think of some ways the movement of goods and people changed because of the railroad and canals.

C. WRIGHT N.Y.

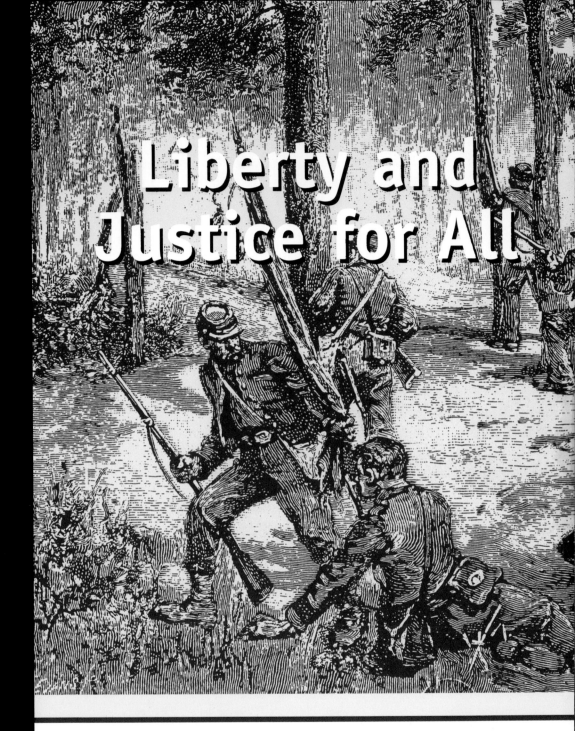

Liberty and Justice for All

timeline of events

1829
The first law is passed requiring children to be educated.

1844
The second New Jersey Constitution is approved.

| 1830 | 1835 | 1840 | 1845 |

1840
Cranberries are first grown in New Jersey.

1847
The telegraph is first used by the Trenton *State Gazette*.

TERMS TO UNDERSTAND
auction
master
plantation
abolitionist
conflict
draft
liberate
emancipation
brigade
asylum
reform
civil rights
amendment
prejudice
labor union

1848
Dorothea Lynde Dix helps open the first hospital for the mentally ill in Trenton.

1855
The first teacher training schools open in Trenton, Paterson, and Newark.

1863
Abraham Lincoln issues the Emancipation Proclamation.

1871
Public schools are made free to all children.

1850 — 1855 — 1860 — 1865 — 1870 — 1875

1850
Steam heat is first used in New Jersey.

1861–1865
The Civil War

1868
The 14th Amendment is added to the Constitution.

1870
The 15th Amendment is added to the Constitution.

139

Slaves were forced to work long hours in the fields.

Slavery

" . . . All men are created equal . . . " These words are found in the Declaration of Independence. However, the word "equal" did not apply to the thousands of slaves in our country.

Slaves were brought to our country from Africa. They did not come to America because they wanted to. They were forced to leave their homelands after being captured and sold. Slave traders sold people for money and goods. The slaves were crowded onto wooden sailing ships and chained together. Many did not survive the terrible journey. There was much death and disease.

When the ocean journey was over, slaves were sold to people who would pay the highest price for them. That kind of sale is called an *auction*. Families were broken up and sold to different owners. The owners became known as *masters*.

In the South, there were very large farms called **plantations**. A great number of people were needed to work in the fields. The owners began to depend on slave workers to keep their plantations going.

There were slaves in New Jersey too. They worked on large farms, as servants in houses, and in mines. Slaves were their master's property, just like his boots, horses, house, and anything else he owned.

An End in Sight

There were many people who believed that slavery was wrong. They believed that everyone was "created equal." In 1804, New Jersey passed a law that said slavery was slowly to come to an end. In 1846 another law was passed which ended slavery once and for all in the state. Any child born in the future would be free.

What do you think?

Why is it important to remember the terrible sad parts of history, such as slavery, as well as the good parts?

Learning to Read

Most slaves were not allowed to learn to read. The owners were afraid that if their slaves learned to read and write they might write to slaves from other areas and unite against the masters. If the slaves could read maps and signs, they might try to escape. Still, many slaves learned to read in secret. Being able to read was a way of saying to the masters, "You can never own my mind."

New Jersey Portrait

Dr. James Still
1812–1882

Dr. Still's father bought his freedom and his mother was a runaway slave. They fled to the Pine Barrens. They were on the run when James was born in Medford. James worked as a woodchopper in the pinelands of New Jersey. He learned to read and soon was reading everything he could find. He studied plants and herbs and learned how he could make medicine to help cure many illnesses. One Sunday, over fifty patients came to his home for treatment. Dr. Still only had three months of schooling and never had a license to practice medicine. Two of his sons went on to become doctors. One was the first African American student to graduate from Harvard Medical School. He once said, "I claim that truthfulness and energy . . . [help] us to [overcome] all difficulties in life . . . and make us prosperous and happy."

The Underground Railroad

When the slaves in the South learned that some states in the North did not allow slavery anymore, many started to run away from the plantations. People who did not believe in slavery and did all they could to have it stopped were called *abolitionists*. Some Quakers were against slavery. Others did what they could to help the cause. Many states had strict laws against anyone helping runaway slaves.

Abolitionists were very busy helping runaway slaves find a safe place to live far away from their masters. They set up a secret system called the Underground Railroad. This "railroad" had no tracks and no engine, but it did have "stations."

The stations were the homes, barns, or other buildings where slaves could hide. Neers Drug Store in Paterson was one of these buildings. Runaway slaves were fed and hidden there during the day. At night, they went on their way again. A "conductor" led them to the next station.

The towns of Camden and New Brunswick were important stops along the way. Some of the runaway slaves remained in New Jersey and other Northern states, but some traveled as far as Canada on their journey to freedom. Thousands of slaves crossed New Jersey on their way to safety.

It was a frightening experience to be a runaway slave. If caught, slaves were whipped or sometimes even killed.

Railroad Signals

There were secret signals used on the Underground Railroad. Quilts were hung on clotheslines to let the conductors know if it was safe or not to bring the "passengers" into the building.

Another signal was a stripe painted on a house. If a runaway slave saw a house with one row of bricks on the chimney painted white, he knew the people in the house were part of the Underground Railroad. It was safe to go inside.

Railroad Helpers

A Quaker by the name of Abigail Goodwin worked very hard to keep the Railroad alive. She went out to beg for money, food, and clothing. She also organized clubs that helped her get these things.

William Still was a "station master" on the Underground Railroad. Dr. James Still was his older brother. He helped many slaves along their route from Philadelphia to Trenton and other towns along the Delaware River. In 1873, all his records about the Underground Railroad were published in a book.

Railroad Tales

Many slaves escaped to freedom on the Underground Railroad, but not all made it. Some people were in the business of catching runaway slaves. They could earn money by returning a slave to his master. The following excerpt is from *Tales from the Underground Railroad* by Kate Connell.

> . . . The dangers of running away were . . . great. Slaveholders were usually rich, powerful people, and the law was on their side. Even in the "free" states like Indiana, a runaway slave was still . . . the property of the owner and if captured had to be returned.
>
> So Seth, Vina, Peter, Levin, and Catharine were put aboard a steamboat in chains, bound for Alabama.
>
> When they reached the plantation, Peter and Levin each got two hundred lashes with the whip, Vina got less than a hundred and Catharine wasn't whipped at all . . . whippings were . . . light punishment.
>
> Seth . . . disappeared from the steam boat . . . his body was found washed up . . . he was buried, still in irons [chains around the ankles] on the river bank.

Some "conductors" had the slaves run away on a Saturday night so they wouldn't be missed until Sunday. The slave's owner couldn't put an ad in the paper until Monday. This gave runaways a two-day head start.

Harriet Tubman

One of the most famous conductors was Harriet Tubman. She was an escaped slave herself. She led over 300 slaves to freedom and did most of her work in southern New Jersey. She even worked in hotels in Cape May to raise money to keep the Railroad running.

Harriet Tubman works on a "signal" quilt. If the quilt was hanging on a clothesline, the slaves knew it was safe to come to that house.

A Nation Divided

Many *conflicts* were dividing the entire country. These conflicts were about freedom and rights.

States' Rights

One conflict was over what rights a state should have. People in the South thought the states should have more power than the national government. They were worried about the government having too much control over them.

People in the North thought the national government should have certain powers over the states. They thought that really important rules should be the same all across the nation.

Slavery

As you know, another important conflict was slavery. Many people, mostly in the South, owned slaves. Many people in the North felt it was wrong for anyone to own another person. Others felt it was up to each state to decide if slavery would be allowed.

There were also other parts of the country trying to become states. Southerners wanted the new states to allow slavery. Northerners wanted the new states to be free.

Economics

Many Southerners said slavery was important to their economy. The crops they grew, such as cotton, tobacco, rice, and sugar needed many fieldworkers. The farmers thought their way of life depended on slavery.

In the North, people worked in other industries. Thousands of people in Northern cities worked in factories. They also worked to build canals and railroads. Some people worked for themselves making barrels, wagons, and other goods for the factory, home, or farm. There were farms, but they were smaller. In most cases the families could do the work themselves.

President Abraham Lincoln thought it was very important that the country stay together under one government. He also felt that the slaves should be freed.

The Civil War

The feelings between the free and slave states were worse than ever in the early 1860s. Soon, the Southern states no longer wanted to belong to the United States of America. They broke away from the Union. They called themselves the Confederate States of America, or the Confederacy.

The Civil War began. This was one of the saddest chapters in America's history. New Jersey had a very important part in it. No Civil War battles were fought on New Jersey soil, but over 85,000 soldiers from New Jersey fought in the Union army. Over 6,000 of them lost their lives.

In Camden, the factories were very busy making boots, shoes, uniforms, cannons, rifles, and ships. The city of Paterson produced engines that were used to pull trains carrying soldiers and supplies to many parts of the country where the war was going on.

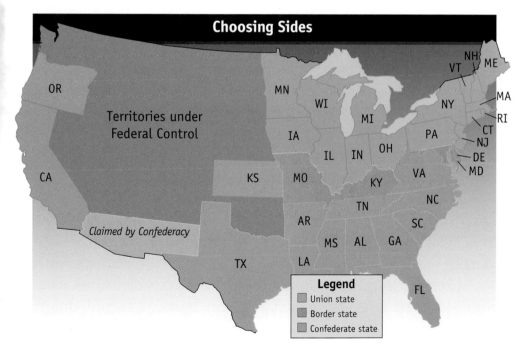

A civil war is a war in which people from the same nation fight each other. The Northern states were called the Union. The Southern states were called the Confederacy.

A Union State

New Jersey was clearly a Union state. However, The South was very important to New Jersey's economy. Many things that were made in New Jersey's factories were sold in the South. Many southern people vacationed in hotels and resorts along the New Jersey shore. Also, many of the students at Princeton University were from Southern states. So, many people in New Jersey were confused about their position in the war. But, in the end, New Jersey was loyal to the Union.

The War Drags On

Both sides thought the war would be short. In the South, soldiers were asked to serve for no more than a year. President Abraham Lincoln asked for even less. He called for soldiers to serve for three months. But the war went on. As it got longer, fewer soldiers signed up. Both sides had to *draft* men to get enough soldiers. The men had to join or go to jail.

What do you think?

Abraham Lincoln was president of the United States during the Civil War. He said, "A house divided against itself cannot stand." What do you think this means?

African Americans in the Union Army

The African American men of the 14th Regiment New Jersey Volunteer Infantry were proud of the fact that they were not drafted but had enlisted of their own free will. The regiment fought for almost three years. The men traveled over 1,000 miles by rail, over 600 miles by ship, and over 2,000 miles by foot.

Former slave Frederick Douglass felt that military service would be a pathway from slavery to full citizenship. He said, "Let the slaves and free colored people be called into service, and formed into a *liberating* army, to march into the South and raise the banner of *emancipation* among the slaves."

By the end of the Civil War, over 185,000 African Americans had volunteered to serve in the Union army and navy. This was about ten percent of the total soldiers from the North.

After viewing the bodies of hundreds of African Americans who lost their lives during a Civil War battle, a white Union officer said:

> "As I looked upon their . . . faces. . . I swore to myself a solemn oath . . . to defend the rights of those men who had given their blood for me and my country and for their race forever."

Charles F. Hopkins, a soldier from Boonton, was being held at Andersonville prison. He escaped but lost his way and couldn't get back to the Union lines. He returned to Andersonville prison by secretly getting himself mixed with a new group of prisoners. He later won a Medal of Honor.

African Americans fought for the North during the Civil War.

A soldier for the Union army stops to rest.

Honorable Soldiers

Sergeant Carney was the first African American to be awarded a Medal of Honor for bravery during the Civil War. He served in Company C, of the 54th Massachusetts Colored Infantry. He grabbed the flag after it was dropped and led the way to the top of the fort's wall and planted it there. After fierce fighting, his troop had to retreat. He brought the flag back to his lines after being wounded twice.

John Lawson from New York was awarded the Medal of Honor for bravery during the Battle of Mobile Bay. He was a gunner on the USS *Hartford*. During the battle, Lawson was wounded in the leg and then thrown against the side of the ship when an enemy shell exploded. He was told to go for medical treatment, but remained at his station until the battle was over.

Charles T. Trowbridge was born in Morristown. He joined in the Union army and later became an officer. It was said that he prayed daily with his men and asked them to think of themselves as equal to all races.

Young Boys Go to War

Most soldiers were at least eighteen years old, but some younger boys went to war as well. In the North, boys as young as nine years old were buglers in the army. Other boys who went to visit their fathers stayed on to fight. Many lied about their age so they could fight in the war.

After the war, the government changed its rules. The Civil War was the last time large numbers of boys so young fought for our country.

Johnny Clem from Newark was a drummer boy in the army. He was nine years old.

Philip Kearny

One important Union general from New Jersey was Philip Kearny. He had a long military career. He fought in the Mexican War and lost his arm. After that he continued to serve in the army. He was a general in the Civil War. He commanded the First New Jersey brigade. He was involved in many battles and was known for his bravery.

During a Civil War battle in Virginia, Kearny ended up behind Confederate lines by mistake. He was told to surrender, but he rode through the enemy's ranks instead. They opened fire and he was killed.

Freedom

President Lincoln tried to end the horrible war. He tried to solve the slavery problem. He offered to pay slave owners for any slaves they would free. Not one state took his offer. Lincoln had even asked the Confederate states to come back into the Union without freeing their slaves. They refused.

Finally, Lincoln issued the Emancipation Proclamation. In this official paper he freed the slaves in the Confederacy. It was a day of great rejoicing. African Americans would be free to build their own lives. They sang "Thank God, I'm free at last!"

Peace at Last

For four long years Americans fought one another. At first the South had won many battles. But the North was better able to fight a long war because their factories could make the things they needed. Finally the South surrendered. The Civil War was over. More than a half million men and women had lost their lives. It was a terrible price to pay, but the country was back together once again.

Education for All

Education in New Jersey had not changed much since the old colonial days. Only children from wealthy families had the opportunity to go to school. Some churches also had schools, but there were many children who were left out. People in New Jersey started to change this. Laws were passed to require all children to go to school.

The first schools were very poor. At first, the teachers knew little more than their students. Soon schools were started to train people who wanted to become teachers. New Jersey schools were soon on their way to becoming what they are today.

Linking the past and the present

How are public schools paid for today? Where does the money come from to pay all the people it takes to run a school?

Clara Barton

Clarissa Barton was born on Christmas Day, 1821. Ever since she could talk, she called herself Clara. When she was eleven, Clara's brother David had an accident. For two years she cared for him, and his health returned. She had a calm way about her that made him feel very restful.

Clara went to live in Bordentown. She got a teaching position in a school where only the wealthy children could attend. She was upset that there was no school for poor children. She opened the first public school in New Jersey, where she worked for free.

During the Civil War, Clara took care of hundreds of Union soldiers. After the war she helped to locate missing soldiers.

In 1881 Clara founded the American Red Cross. For over twenty-five years she worked without pay. Today the Red Cross has almost two million volunteers working in the United States.

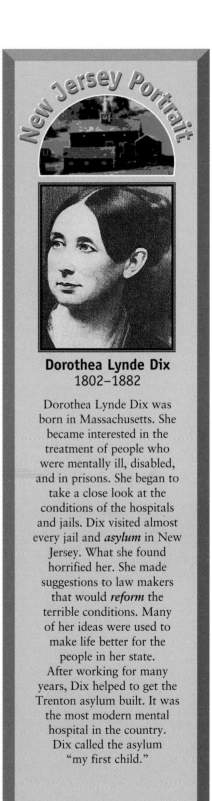

New Jersey Portrait

Dorothea Lynde Dix
1802–1882

Dorothea Lynde Dix was born in Massachusetts. She became interested in the treatment of people who were mentally ill, disabled, and in prisons. She began to take a close look at the conditions of the hospitals and jails. Dix visited almost every jail and *asylum* in New Jersey. What she found horrified her. She made suggestions to law makers that would *reform* the terrible conditions. Many of her ideas were used to make life better for the people in her state. After working for many years, Dix helped to get the Trenton asylum built. It was the most modern mental hospital in the country. Dix called the asylum "my first child."

Reconstruction

It was a new world for African Americans at the end of the Civil War. The time was known as the Reconstruction Period, or the time of rebuilding. It was now possible for African Americans to make their own choices, go where they wanted, and be what they wanted to be. Reading and writing were always important, and now the people had a chance to get the education they deserved.

Freedmen's Bureau

Freedom brought some new problems to the country. After the war, thousands of African Americans and whites were without homes. Soon there was some relief. It was called the Freedmen's Bureau. This agency tried to solve the problems of the unemployed, sick, and homeless. Most centers were set up in the South because of the large amount of destruction there.

However, some people in the North thought that too much government money was being spent to help African Americans. There were Southerners who didn't like the idea that African Americans were being helped at all.

One of the things the Bureau did was to see that African Americans were paid for their work. This was a hard thing for the ex-slave owner to accept. Now he had to pay for the fields to be plowed or the factories to be operated.

The Freedmen's Bureau issued funds and coupons to freed slaves.

Legal Equality

Thaddeus Stevens, a politician from the North, suggested that two bills be voted upon and made into laws. The first would keep the Freedmen's Bureau open. The other would guarantee that African Americans would have *civil rights* just like white citizens.

This would be known as the 14th *Amendment* to the Constitution. After many months of debating, the 14th Amendment was approved.

Right after the 14th Amendment came the 15th, which said, "The right of the citizens of the United States to vote shall not be denied . . . on account of race, color or previous condition of servitude." This meant that African Americans and former slaves could now vote and send people to Congress to speak for them.

Problems Remain

When the Union army returned to the North, riots started to break out in the South. An organization made up of angry white men called themselves the Ku Klux Klan. Members started to beat and kill many African Americans. When this started, many more African Americans moved North to find jobs and start new lives for themselves and their families.

Ku Klux Klan

Even though they were free and protected by the law, many African Americans still met with *prejudice*. They were not allowed to join any white *labor unions* that protected the rights of the workers. When this happened, many African Americans started their own labor unions.

The Emancipation Proclamation and other reforms helped many African Americans. But, even though they were free from slavery, they still had a hard time gaining equality and civil rights.

What do you think?

The problems of race and prejudice still challenge us today.
- **Have you experienced prejudice in your life? How did you feel?**
- **How can you and your family and friends be more tolerant of people who are different from you?**

Liberty and Justice for All

Cause and Effect

Whenever we do something there is an effect, or result. For example, when we enter a dark room and flip on the light switch, the room is filled with light. This is called cause and effect. The cause is flipping on the light switch. The effect is that the room is filled with light. Life is filled with cause-and-effect relationships.

As we study New Jersey history it is important to understand cause and effect. This will give us a better picture of our history.

CAUSE: Something that happened first, and caused something else to happen

EFFECT: What happened as a result of the cause

Look at each pair of sentences below. On a separate piece of paper, write 'C' for the cause and 'E' for the effect. Look back in the chapter if you need help.

EXAMPLE:

<u>C</u> Abraham Lincoln issued the Emancipation Proclamation.

<u>E</u> Slaves were freed.

1. _____ Farmers in the South planted huge crops of cotton.

   _____ They needed workers to pick the cotton.

2. _____ A slave girl was caught learning to read.

   _____ She was punished by the master.

3. _____ Some slaves made it to freedom.

   _____ Brave people risked their lives to escape from slavery.

4. _____ The Trenton mental hospital was built.

   _____ Dorothea Lynde Dix worked to reform the treatment of the mentally ill.

5. _____ School was not free to everyone.

   _____ Many children did not have the chance to get an education.

6. _____ The Freedmen's Bureau was set up to help African Americans.

   _____ After emancipation, it was still hard for African Americans to be treated equally.

Chapter 9 Review

1. Why did farmers in the Southern states want to own slaves?
2. Why did people think that slavery was wrong?
3. What was the Underground Railroad?
4. How long did the Civil War last?
5. What was the role of the Freedmen's Bureau?
6. What agency did Clara Barton found?
7. What does the 14th Amendment say?
8. What does the 15th Amendment say?

Geography Tie-In

Look at the map on page 145. Use the map key to figure out what kinds of states surrounded New Jersey. Were they Union states, border states, Confederate states? What kinds of problems might the "border states" have faced?

An overseer made sure slaves were working hard in the fields.

THE TIME
1869–1913

PEOPLE TO KNOW
U.S. President Grover Cleveland
Pietro Botto
Maria Botto
Elizabeth Gurley Flynn
Clara Maass

PLACES TO LOCATE
Ireland
Russia
Poland
Germany
Italy
Greece
France
Hungary
Philippines
Ellis Island
Liberty Island
Madison
Summit
Bayonne
Wharton
Franklin
Haledon
East Orange
Belleville
Caldwell

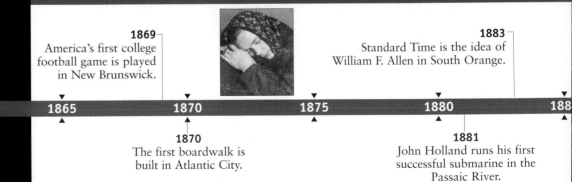

timeline of events

1869 America's first college football game is played in New Brunswick.

1870 The first boardwalk is built in Atlantic City.

1883 Standard Time is the idea of William F. Allen in South Orange.

1881 John Holland runs his first successful submarine in the Passaic River.

1865 1870 1875 1880 188

10

New Jersey's Part in the American Dream

TERMS TO UNDERSTAND
immigrant
famine
steerage
persecute
tradition
sweatshop
strike
tenement
variety

The Statue of Liberty welcomes people to America. (Photo by Tom Till)

1895
Mary Philbrook becomes the first female lawyer in the state.

1913
Mill workers go on strike in Paterson.

| 1890 | 1895 | 1900 | 1905 | 1910 | 1915 |

1889
Many large companies open in New Jersey.

1908
Botto House is constructed in Haledon.

155

Immigration

A T THE END OF THE NINETEENTH CENTURY, millions of *immigrants* came to our country. Why would so many people leave their homes and families and risk a dangerous trip across the ocean?

The people who came here were looking for a better life. Some who came were looking for a place where they could be free to follow their own religious beliefs. Others left their homelands because of war. Some came because in America there was land and the promise of jobs. Some immigrants had to leave their countries simply to survive. In Ireland there was a *famine*. People were starving. Russian, Polish, and German Jews left because the government was driving them out—mainly because of their religious beliefs. People throughout Europe had heard stories about America. They called it the "land of opportunity."

By Foot, by Train, by Ship

No matter what country they came from, the people had a long journey ahead of them. Just to leave their homelands they had to walk great distances or take trains to get to the nearest port. Then they often had to wait days or weeks for the next ship.

On the ship there was not much to eat. Many people were seasick. The ships moved slowly, taking several weeks to reach America.

Arriving in America

Near the Statue of Liberty was a place called Castle Garden. Here the immigrants were examined. Doctors made sure that they were not carrying any diseases. Officers checked to see if they were wanted by the police in their own country. Some people were sent back to their countries. Others made it through the inspection.

In 1892, the government decided it needed a larger place to examine the thousands of immigrants coming into New York and New Jersey. The new place was called Ellis Island where an average of 3,000 people a day were inspected.

Top Five Reasons People Come to America

1. To escape poverty and poor living conditions.
2. To enjoy the freedoms of democracy.
3. To escape war.
4. To practice the religion of their choice.
5. To join other family members.

The New Jersey Adventure

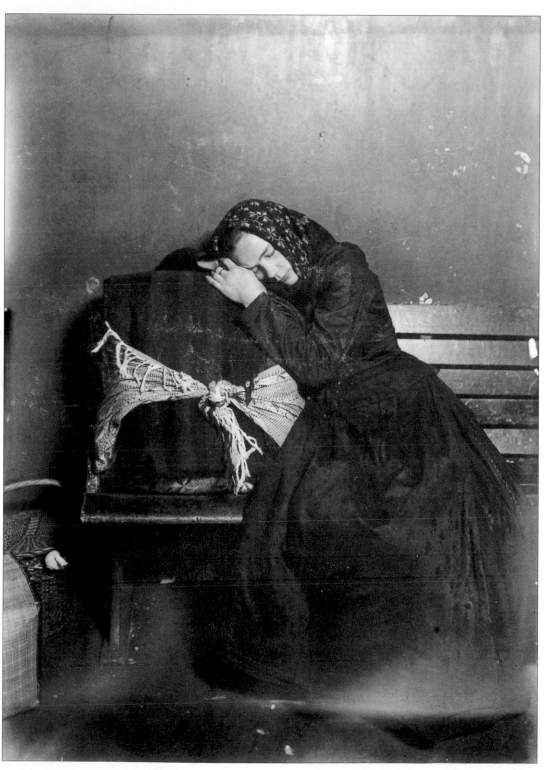

The journey to America was long and hard.

New Jersey's Part in the American Dream

Journey to America

Many of the immigrants who came to America could only afford the least expensive steamship ticket. This was called a *steerage* ticket. The ticket allowed a person to stay at the bottom level of the ship. People stayed next to the engine room, where it was hot and noisy.

Rosa Cristoforo sailed to America from Sicily. Sicily is a large island off of Italy. She was sailing to New York to meet her husband, Santino. Here is an excerpt from her diary:

All of us poor people had to go down through a hole to the bottom of the ship. There was a big dark room down there with rows of wooden shelves all around where we were going to sleep—the Italian, the German, the Polish, the Swede, the French—every kind. . . . When the dinner bell rang we were all standing in line holding . . . tin plates . . . waiting for soup and bread.

Nicholas Gerros was born in Greece. When he was about fourteen he left his country and sailed for America. That was in 1900. When he was ninety, he told about his journey to America:

Six of us kids all about fourteen spent a week in Naples (Italy), then after two weeks and a bit seasick we unloaded at Castle Garden. There we got an eye exam. Some man came along. He gave us a box of food. In the box there was a banana. We didn't know how to eat it. We'd never seen bananas. Finally somebody realized that and showed us.

Some immigrants came from other parts of Europe. Mary Antin was one of thousands of Russian Jews who left her country because they were being persecuted. They were not allowed to practice their religion freely. Her journey was much longer than usual:

> For sixteen days the ship was our world. . . . I would imagine myself all alone on the ocean . . . sometimes . . . I was aware of no human presence . . . only the sea and sky. I felt as if I found a friend.
>
> Now imagine yourself parting with [leaving] all you love . . . breaking up your home, selling the things . . . dear to you; starting on a journey without experience in travelling . . . forced to go and make friends with strangers . . . suffering the miseries of seasickness. How would you feel?
>
> Oh, it's our turn at last. We are questioned, examined, and dismissed! . . . the long journey is at an END!

Not all people thought steerage areas were bad. A Swedish lady had quite a different experience in 1899:

> We came over in the steerage . . . The voyage wasn't bad. They give people beds in the steerage now, and all their food, and it is very good and well cooked. It took us twelve days to cross the sea . . . people got over the seasickness . . . there was plenty of dancing . . . most people in the steerages were Swedes and very pleasant and friendly. On fine days we could walk outside on the deck. Two men had concertinas and one had a violin.

Statue of Liberty Facts

- Original name:
  Liberty Enlightening the World
- Island's original name:
  Bedloe's Island
- Island's current name:
  Liberty Island (name changed during World War I)
- Statue's height: 151 feet
- Base height: 154 feet
- Total height: 305 feet

A Statue's Skin

The copper that makes up the Statue of Liberty's "skin" came from a copper mine on a small island in Norway. It took 176,368 pounds of copper to cover the Statue of Liberty.

Building Lady Liberty

Before the immigrants stepped on shore, they were greeted by the sight of one of the largest statues ever built—the Statue of Liberty. It stands on Liberty Island in New Jersey waters.

The Statue of Liberty has been a welcome symbol for millions of immigrants. She was a gift to our country from France. The gift was to celebrate America's 100th birthday. On October 28, 1886, the Statue of Liberty was unveiled before a huge crowd that included President Grover Cleveland.

A man from Hungary wrote:

A well-dressed man who spoke our language told us that the big iron woman in the harbor was a goddess that gave out liberty freely and without cost to everybody. He said the thing in her hand that looked like a broom was light—that it was to give us light and liberty too . . . he told us a man could stand inside the broom.

Struggling in a New Land

When the immigrants arrived, they usually settled in cities and neighborhoods that were already filled with people from their homeland. There they could speak the language of their home country. They could keep their *traditions*. Cities in New Jersey started to have neighborhoods like Little Italy, Little Hungary, and Little Slovakia.

Making a Living

In the 1880s the factory worker's life was very hard. The day started at six in the morning and usually ended at six in the evening. The shops were very hot and noisy with the clatter of machines. Children as young as seven years old could be found working next to adults. Many workers ate their lunches by their machines and had to ask permission to go to the bathroom. Some families also worked at home. The home businesses were sometimes called *sweatshops*. Can you guess why?

Immigrants Help New Jersey Grow		
Where They Came From	**Where They Worked**	**Cities They Worked In**
Italy, Poland, Czechoslovakia, and Russia	Factories	Newark, Passaic, Jersey City, and Paterson
Hungary, Poland	Clay Pits	Perth Amboy and New Brunswick
Italy	Greenhouses and Gardens	Madison, Morristown, and Summit
Poland	Oil Refineries	Bayonne
Hungary	Mills and Mines	Wharton and Franklin

Children often sold newspapers to make money for their families.

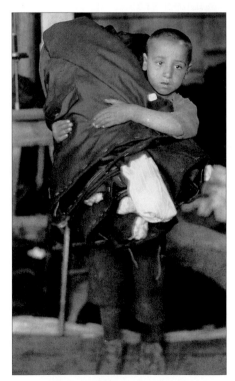

Working children were common everywhere. Children eight or ten years old worked in factories, warehouses, laundries, and stores.

Child Labor

Children often had to work in order for families to pay rent and buy food. Girls worked in textile mills at spinning machines. They also worked as "cash girls" in department stores. They gave change to the customers. By 1900, both women and girls were working in many industries, making everything from art tiles to wool coats.

Boys ran errands and made deliveries for the druggist, printer, mill owner, and grocer. If boys were not working in factories, they were often out on the streets selling newspapers or shining shoes.

In 1875, New Jersey passed a law that every child between the ages of eight and fourteen had to go to school at least twelve weeks a year. Today every child between the ages of seven and sixteen years of age must attend school for thirty-five weeks each year. One of the main reasons why children were rescued from a life of working in factories, sweatshops, and on the streets was that they had to be in school part of the time.

By 1900, although some states had laws that protected child workers, it was very difficult to enforce them. Then Congress passed a law that said no company could ship goods made by child labor. Factory owners had to check the birth certificates of all young people who applied for jobs. About twenty years later, Congress passed a law that said children had to be at least sixteen before they could work all day.

By 1915, New Jersey, along with thirty-two other states, said children had to go to school until age sixteen.

What do you think?

Do you think children should be in school instead of working to help support their families? How would an education help them be better workers when they grow up?

Problems on the Job

Some people who had started the new industries became rich. They lived in huge houses and dressed in expensive clothes. But the people who worked in the factories got low wages.

There were few laws in those days that said how factory workers should be treated. Many factory owners did not care much about the workers. They did not try to give them a nice place to work. They pushed them to make more. They pushed them to work faster. The people worked twelve or more hours a day in factories that were often unsafe and unhealthy. They were paid very low wages.

If anyone complained, he or she was fired. There were so many other people looking for jobs that the owners could easily find someone else.

Workers began to come together and fight for change. Workers formed unions. One way workers tried to change poor working conditions was to go on *strike*. They refused to work until they got more money and safer workplaces.

This young woman worked ten hours a day in a factory that made cloth. She was sixteen years old.

What do you think?

Most businesses have an eight-hour workday. Many people work more.

- Do you think eight hours is too long or too short for adults to be at work?
- Talk to adults you know about some problems at work today. How can we make places of work better?

Botto House

Just like many immigrants, Pietro and Maria Botto left their home in Italy and came to America. Their hopes and dreams were not only for themselves, but also for their children. They built a house in Haledon.

In Italy, the Botto family had been silk workers. They brought that skill with them to America. They soon found out that factories in Paterson were dirty, noisy, and did not have enough fresh air to breathe. Also, the hours were long and the pay was hardly enough to feed and clothe their family and pay the rent. Vacations and the few extra things that would make life a little more enjoyable were not possible for most of the workers. There were thousands of factory workers having the same problems.

One day in 1913, about 25,000 silk workers in Paterson did not go to work. They held a strike. They refused to work

A workers' rally at the Botto home, 1913. Find the speaker on the balcony.
Can you guess how many people are at this rally?
What do you think the speaker is going to talk about?

The New Jersey Adventure

until the factories were changed for the better. The striking workers gathered at Pietro Botto's home. They listened to long speeches made from the balcony. They also sang songs about the strike.

In 1974, the Botto house became a National Historic Site. In 1982 it became a National Historic Landmark. Many people visit it from all parts of the world.

Mrs. Bunny Kuiken, a granddaughter of Pietro Botto, said:

I vow [promise] not to let people forget. . . . When I was a child, a favorite pastime at our house was looking at old family photographs. I was intrigued [fascinated] by one picture in particular, showing thousands of people looking up at someone addressing them from the balcony of our house in Haledon. . . .

Paterson Strike

At the silk mills in Paterson, owners wanted weavers to run four looms instead of just two. The weavers said this was too hard. Neither side was willing to do what the other wanted. So, the workers walked off the job.

Three groups were involved in the strike: silk weavers, ribbon weavers, and people who dyed the cloth. All were working in dangerous surroundings. They were asked to do too much. The ten-hour day and the use of child labor were also concerns of the workers.

Women could be found in almost every textile department except the dye house. They were usually paid less than men. The hourly pay for men and women ranged from three to five cents per hour. Children often received two or three cents per hour.

After six months, the workers had to go back to work because their money had run out. It took a little while, but in time all the things they were striking for were given to them by the factory owners. After the strike, the workers worked a fifty-five instead of a sixty-hour week. They earned between three cents and nine cents an hour.

Silk for the Rich

Members of an organization known as the Industrial Workers of the World (IWW) frequently met at Botto House during the strike. One of the IWW leaders was Elizabeth Gurley Flynn. She was very popular among the women.

Here is a quote from Elizabeth:

The textile workers do not wear either woolen or silk while rich people wear both. I asked, "Do you wear silk?" They answered in a lively chorus: "No!" I asked: "Does your mother wear silk?" Again there was a loud, "No!" But a child's voice interrupted, making a statement. This is what he said, "My mother has a silk dress. My father spoiled the cloth and had to bring it home." The silk worker had to pay for the piece he spoiled and only then did his wife get a silk dress!

Clara Maass
1876–1901

Clara Maass was from East Orange. During the Spanish-American War, she served as a nurse. She helped to care for thousands of wounded soldiers. She was discharged from the army and a few months later served in the Philippines. While she was there she learned about a terrible disease called yellow fever. She volunteered for experiments to try to find its cause. Doctors thought that the mosquito was the cause, but they needed volunteers to allow themselves to be bitten. Clara Maass stepped forward and allowed herself to be bitten. The first time, she became slightly ill. Then she allowed herself to be bitten a second time. This time she died. Then the doctors knew for sure that the mosquito was the deadly carrier of yellow fever. Today a hospital in Belleville is named after her.

Living Conditions

Some immigrants lived in overcrowded *tenements* (apartment houses) with many other families. After returning from their backbreaking jobs at night, people often slept on the floor. There were outhouses behind the buildings. Later, when indoor plumbing was added, the only bathroom was located in a hallway and used by everyone in the building. There was usually only one sink.

Many Contributions

Many immigrants brought special skills and talents to America. They added *variety* to this country. They helped build New Jersey and the whole country. It took intelligence, new ideas, and a strong body to make the American dream work for immigrants. Many immigrants added to the world of music, art, engineering, science, literature, food, and fashion.

What do you think?

America is often called the great "melting pot." This nickname describes how people from different backgrounds and cultures "melted" together to form one country and one culture.

Some people prefer to think of America as a "tossed salad." Each tomato or cucumber is different, but they all add to the salad, giving it more flavor. Different cultures keep some of their own traditions, while becoming part of an American tradition.

What do you think? Is America more like a melting pot or a tossed salad?

New Jersey is made up of people from many different backgrounds.

▲ Photo by Walter Choroszewski

In older tenements, there was a sink and faucet in the hallway and people had to fetch their own water.

New Jersey's Part in the American Dream

Having Fun

The late 1800s and early 1900s were a time of great struggle and great change. But this was also a time of great fun. People listened to the radio and went to movies. Baseball games became popular. Every small town had its own team. Many companies also had teams. Bicycle races and roller skating were also popular.

First Football Game

Imagine two football teams on the field with twenty-five players on each side. There were no helmets, shoulder pads, or equipment. That's the way the game was played back in 1869. Two colleges, Rutgers and Princeton, played the first game in New Brunswick.

The ball was round and made of rubber. You could score points for your team by kicking the ball or hitting it with your fist across a goal line. The defending team could try to stop the other team by tackling the players to the ground. Rutgers won the very first game by a score of six to four.

Activity

What Would You Bring?

Pretend you are moving to a foreign country. You must travel like immigrants did 200 years ago. You can't pack much. You will be sailing on a boat with hundreds of strangers. There is hardly room for you, let alone your things. You must carry everything you take with you.

What do you choose? Imagine that you have a grocery bag. You can only take five things and they must all fit in the bag. What will you bring? Write down the five items you chose and why you chose them.

Chapter 10 Review

1. List three reasons why immigrants came to America.

2. Describe the journey an immigrant had to make from Europe to New Jersey.

3. Describe the conditions on a steerage ticket.

4. What jobs did immigrants commonly do in New Jersey?

5. How did workers change poor working conditions?

6. What was unique about Grover Cleveland's presidency?

Geography Tie-In

1. On a map of the world, find all the countries listed in the chapter that immigrants came from.

2. On a map of New Jersey, find the cities and towns that the immigrants settled in.

THE TIME
1879-1945

PEOPLE TO KNOW
Thomas Edison
U.S. President
  Woodrow Wilson
Mary Philbrook
U.S. President Franklin
  Roosevelt
Anne Frank
Albert Einstein

PLACES TO LOCATE
Menlo Park
West Orange
Europe
Paterson
Dover
Mays Landing
Belcoville
Newark
Camden
Kearny
Elizabeth
Hoboken
Jersey City
Passaic
Hawaii
Fort Dix
Germany

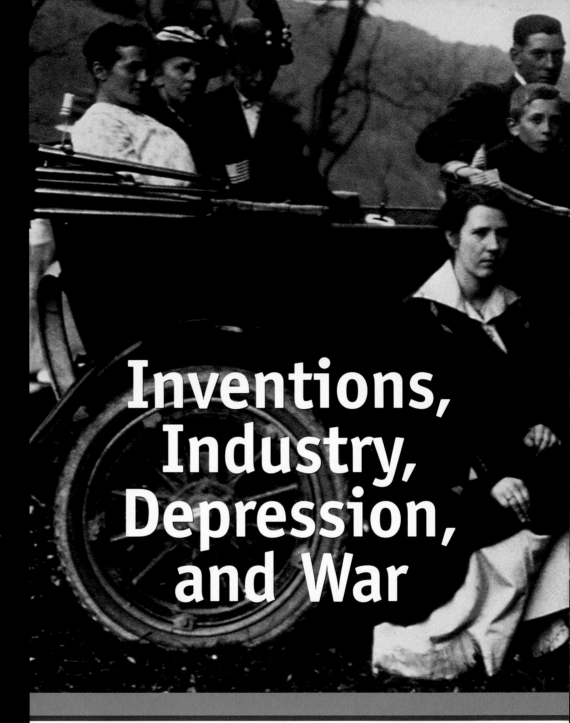

Inventions, Industry, Depression, and War

timeline of events

1880

1879
Edison invents the light bulb.

1889
Edison perfects the motion picture.

1890

1892
The automobile is invented.

1895
Radio is invented.

1900

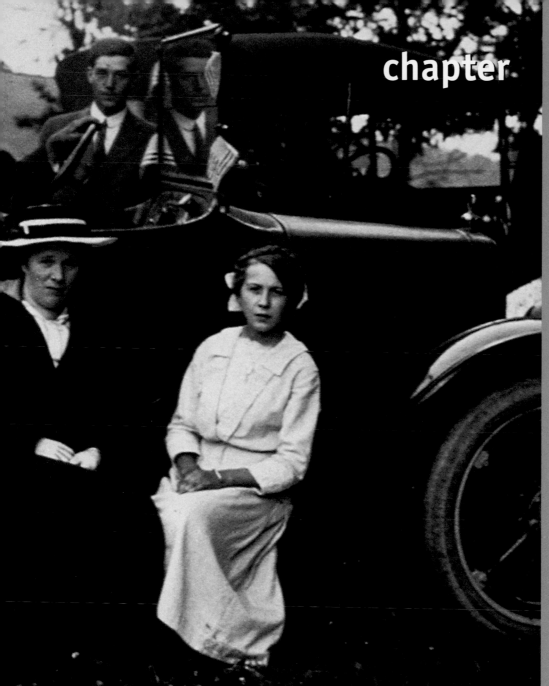

TERMS TO UNDERSTAND
generator
patent
civilian
woolens
embarkation
suffrage
consumer
generation
prohibit
stock
ration
fatigues
Holocaust
concentration camp
atom

Family outings in cars were a new kind of fun in the 1920s.

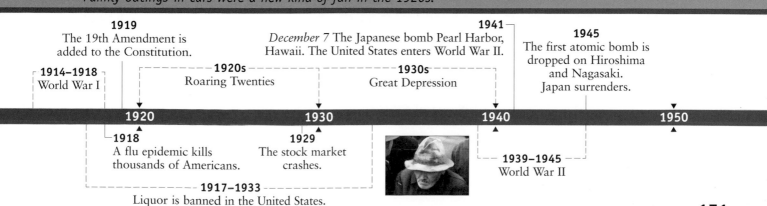

1919
The 19th Amendment is
added to the Constitution.

1941
December 7 The Japanese bomb Pearl Harbor,
Hawaii. The United States enters World War II.

1945
The first atomic bomb is
dropped on Hiroshima
and Nagasaki.
Japan surrenders.

1914–1918
World War I

1920s
Roaring Twenties

1930s
Great Depression

1920   1930   1940   1950

1918
A flu epidemic kills
thousands of Americans.

1929
The stock market
crashes.

1939–1945
World War II

1917–1933
Liquor is banned in the United States.

Telephones changed the way people communicated.

The whole family liked to gather around to hear the radio.

A Time of Change

WE HAVE SEEN HOW NEW JERSEY changed during the nineteenth century. It would change even more during the next one hundred years. As the new century began, immigrants poured into the state. Cities grew. The country went to war. People in New Jersey and all across the United States faced good times and bad times.

Inventions Make Life Easier

Electricity

Many inventions changed people's lives. Electric *generators* were one of the most important. They changed the way people worked, played, and lived.

Generators are machines that make electricity. They made electric lights possible. Electric streetcars ran through cities and towns. New machines that used electricity were invented. There were electric washing machines, irons, stoves, refrigerators, and vacuum cleaners.

Telephones

Alexander Graham Bell, who had invented the telephone many years before, was now able to talk with other people from coast to coast. People in New Jersey could make local calls before 1900, but it took another thirty years before nearly all homes and businesses had phone service.

Radio

One of the most exciting inventions was the radio. Everyone across the United States wanted a radio. At first there were not enough to go around. People visited friends who were lucky enough to own one. They gathered around to listen to their favorite programs. They were amazed. Imagine hearing voices and music that came from the air!

Movies

The first movies were silent. Someone played a piano in the theater to go along with the movie. The music got faster and louder when the movie's action got more exciting. Then people figured out how to add sound. The new "talkies" were a hit. Going to a movie cost about twenty-five cents for adults and ten cents for children. At first movie theaters were small, but soon fancy theaters were built.

Linking the past and the present

What influence do movies and radio have on our society today? What influence do they have on your life?

Automobiles

The first automobiles cost about $500. The price was reasonable, and many people bought them. The first cars came in only a few styles and colors. Henry Ford owned the factory that made Ford cars in Michigan. He joked that people could have any color of car they wanted, as long as it was black.

Changing Times, Changing Needs

Before automobiles, horses and mules and other work animals were used for transportation. Horses were kept in stables. Stable owners fed them, brushed them, and provided them with stalls to sleep in. Blacksmiths made horseshoes. In other shops, saddles, harnesses, and wagons were made and sold. With the new automobile, those businesses were not needed as much. New ones were needed. What were some of them?

Can you think of other things that changed because of the automobile? Here are some hints: vacations, jobs, land next to the roads, movement of products, and even sports.

Some people did not like the new "horseless carriage." As drivers went by, people sometimes shouted, "Get a horse!"

EDISON'S INVENTIONS

Thomas Alva Edison is one of the world's greatest inventors. His inventions affected many people and helped shape our society. The light bulb is perhaps his most important invention. How many light bulbs have you used today?

Thomas Edison was born in Ohio in 1847. When he started school, he was thought to be a dull student. Thomas's teacher told his mother that he could not learn. His mother decided to teach him at home.

Tom was taught to learn things for himself. Before he was twelve years old, he had already read many of the works of Shakespeare, Dickens, and other famous writers. His mother gave him a science book for beginners when he was nine. It was filled with chemistry experiments. He ended up doing every single one of them. He fell in love with chemistry.

Edison built his first lab when he was ten years old, but his father didn't care for the idea so much. He tried to get Thomas to spend more time reading and gave him a penny every time he went back to reading books. Thomas obeyed his father, but spent every penny he got to buy more chemicals. Just to be sure no one would get hurt from any of the chemicals in the bottles, he labeled them all **"POISON!"**

At age twelve, Thomas got a job on a local train selling newspapers and candy. He also started his own newspaper. He called it the *Grand Trunk Herald*. Guess where all his money went? If you said chemicals and books, you were right. He was given permission to move his laboratory from his home to a baggage car on the train. One day the train moved suddenly and the chemicals spilled, causing a fire. The conductor was so angry that when the train stopped, he threw Edison and all his chemicals off the train.

When he was fifteen, Thomas tried to jump onto a moving train. Someone grabbed him by his ears to help him up. He felt something snap inside his head and ever

▲ Photo by Tom Till

since that time, he had hearing problems. He could have had the problem solved with an operation. But, he felt that the hearing loss helped him to focus more on his work.

When he was in his late twenties, Thomas Edison moved to Newark, where he made improvements on the typewriter. About five years later he built his new "invention factory" as he called it, in Menlo Park. He had two partners. At one time he had over forty projects going at the same time. He was there for over ten years. During that time he applied for over 3,000 *patents*.

In 1876 Edison started the Edison Electric Light Company. Today it is known as General Electric. After spending $40,000 and doing about 1,200 experiments, he invented the light bulb.

Thomas Alva Edison, 1847–1931

Edison's lab in West Orange is a National Historic Site you can visit.

Soon Edison was known as the "Wizard of Menlo Park." There he invented the phonograph. The first musical recording made on a phonograph was "Mary Had a Little Lamb."

In 1887, a new laboratory was built in West Orange. It was about ten times larger that the one in Menlo Park. Thousands of new inventions were created in that laboratory.

Three days after Edison died, the electric lights throughout the United States were dimmed for one minute in his memory.

World War I

Soon after the new century began, a war started. The fighting involved so many countries that it was called a "world war." At first it was called "The Great War," but years later it became known as World War I. On one side were the Central Powers. They included Germany and Austria-Hungary. On the other side were England, France, Russia, and the United States. They were the Allied Powers. World War I claimed the lives of 10 million people.

Joining the Allies

When the war started in Europe, the United States wanted to stay out of it. President Woodrow Wilson tried to get the countries to stop fighting and live in peace. But, he was not successful. Something happened that made the United States get involved. German submarines sank American ships. After that, the United States joined the Allies.

People who were not soldiers helped by buying war bonds. Bonds were paper certificates. This gave the government money to use to pay for the war. After the war, the people could trade in their war bonds for more money than they had paid for them.

While the men were gone to fight the war, their families had more work to do. Boys from the cities helped farmers harvest their crops. Women made hospital supplies at Red Cross centers. They learned to cook without wheat or meat so those foods could be sent to Europe to feed the soldiers. Children planted gardens and made items for the Red Cross.

BOYS and GIRLS!
You can Help your Uncle Sam Win the War

W.S.S.

Save your Quarters
BUY WAR SAVINGS STAMPS

"We . . . advanced seven miles in one day . . . the men were doing this on empty stomachs and tired, very tired bodies and legs. The men, some of them, drank from the puddles in the roads."

—Lieutenant H. H. Heliwell, United States Ninth Infantry

Since the war was fought in Europe, many farms there were destroyed. *Civilians* as well as soldiers needed food and other farm products. New Jersey farmers helped. They sent some of their crops overseas.

Linking the past and the present

Where do you see the Red Cross and other relief organizations working today? What are they doing in those places?

Girl Scouts collected peach pits for the war effort. The pits were turned into charcoal, which was used in gas masks to filter out deadly gas.

Woodrow Wilson
1856–1924

Woodrow Wilson was born in Virginia. As a young man, he attended the College of New Jersey. He was very involved in public speaking and writing. Music was an important part of his life as a child. He continued to make music an important part of his life when he had a family of his own.

Wilson served as president of Princeton University and governor of New Jersey. He was a leader in reforms. He fought against big companies that were not doing business fairly. He also worked to improve workers' rights.

Wilson became the twenty-eighth president of the United States. He tried to keep the country out of World War I. Unfortunately, the United States did enter the war. Wilson is known for getting the United States more involved in world affairs. He received the Nobel Peace Prize in 1919.

New Jersey Does Its Part

New Jersey factories were busy manufacturing guns, clothing, automobiles, trucks, and almost anything that was needed in the war. Workers in towns such as Paterson, Dover, Mays Landing, and Belcoville worked day and night to help keep the army and navy supplied with equipment. Shipbuilding became a major industry. Ships were built in towns such as Newark, Camden, and Kearny. Submarines were made very quickly.

The Singer Sewing Machine Company in Elizabeth stopped making sewing machines and started making parts for weapons and equipment. Textile plants in Passaic County made *woolens* for blankets and uniforms. Hoboken was a busy shipping center.

The war ended on November 11, 1918. The United States and the Allies won. There were about 150,000 men from New Jersey who served in World War I. Approximately 3,000 of those men died either in battle or from disease.

Ships were built in New Jersey to help win World War I.

What do you think?

World War I was known as "the war to end all wars." Has that turned out to be true?

Spotlight on Hoboken

Hoboken was a very important city during World War I. Hoboken had many German people at the time. Since the United States was fighting Germany, the government watched Hoboken very carefully. Soldiers guarded the piers and patrolled the streets. Some restaurants even stopped serving German food.

Hoboken was also the major point of *embarkation* for soldiers going to Europe. Forty percent of all soldiers sent to Europe went through Hoboken. Since soldiers were leaving for possibly a long time, there were many last-minute marriages in Hoboken. There were as many as forty marriages a day.

These women were called suffragettes. They worked to get the law changed so women could vote.

Votes for Women

After World War I, there were many major changes in our state and across the country. One of the most important changes affected women. The 19th Amendment was added to the United States Constitution. With this new amendment, women got the right to vote. Women called "suffragettes" led the fight for women's *suffrage*. Their success with voting rights led many women to fight for even more rights. Mary Philbrook, a lawyer from Jersey City, spent years helping women win the right to vote.

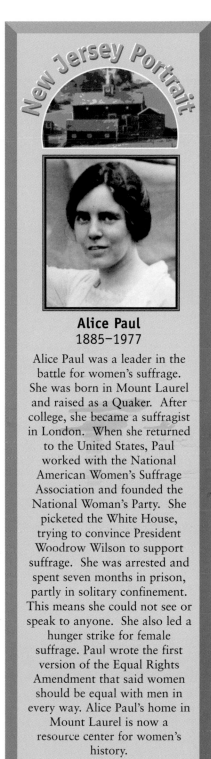

New Jersey Portrait

Alice Paul
1885–1977

Alice Paul was a leader in the battle for women's suffrage. She was born in Mount Laurel and raised as a Quaker. After college, she became a suffragist in London. When she returned to the United States, Paul worked with the National American Women's Suffrage Association and founded the National Woman's Party. She picketed the White House, trying to convince President Woodrow Wilson to support suffrage. She was arrested and spent seven months in prison, partly in solitary confinement. This means she could not see or speak to anyone. She also led a hunger strike for female suffrage. Paul wrote the first version of the Equal Rights Amendment that said women should be equal with men in every way. Alice Paul's home in Mount Laurel is now a resource center for women's history.

New fashions and dances were part of the Roaring Twenties.

The Roaring Twenties

After the war ended, Americans returned from Europe. They wanted to forget the war. People who had lived with shortages wanted to live well. Factories switched from making war materials to making goods for *consumers*. People wanted to buy the new products they saw in store windows. There was plenty of work for everyone and people were spending money freely. Many businesses were allowing their customers to purchase things on a "buy now, pay later" basis.

Before the twenties, people had lived according to a very strict set of rules. Then many of the rules started changing. For example, women were going into careers that had been only open to men.

A new type of music called jazz became very popular along with new types of lively dances such as the "Charleston" and "Ball in the Jack." Clothing styles changed to be more comfortable. Long coats made from the skins of raccoons called "coon skin coats" were very popular for men. For the first time in America, women cut their hair short and wore shorter dresses.

Some very tall buildings called "skyscrapers" were built. Concrete and steel were being used more and more each day. The Holland Tunnel was built to connect New York City and Jersey City. Newark Airport was started. There was a construction boom in the whole country.

Highways were improved. City streets were noisy. They were filled with the sounds of automobiles, busses, trolley cars, and even a few horses and wagons.

What do you think?

What do you think people in the future will say about the styles and fashions of today? What do your clothes, music, and hairstyles say about your *generation*?

Prohibition

The 1920s were a time of fun, but they were also a time of crime and violence. One reason was because of liquor. In 1917 liquor was outlawed in the United States. Those who still wanted to drink went to "speakeasies," or clubs where they could buy liquor. Gangsters often supplied the liquor. "Bootlegging" (secretly buying and selling liquor) became big business.

The liquor law was called Prohibition, because the law *prohibited* making or selling alcohol. The law did not last long. Liquor was made legal again in 1933.

The Great Depression

A depression is a time when most people can't make enough money to take care of their families. They want to work, but they can't find jobs. The depression of the 1930s was the worst depression the United States has ever known. That is why it is called the Great Depression.

"A bad night to be out . . . even if you have warm clothes . . . most of the men don't. Perhaps one in twenty has gloves . . . perhaps two in five have some sort of an overcoat . . . with the buttons missing . . . held together with one hand . . ."

—Bruce Bliven

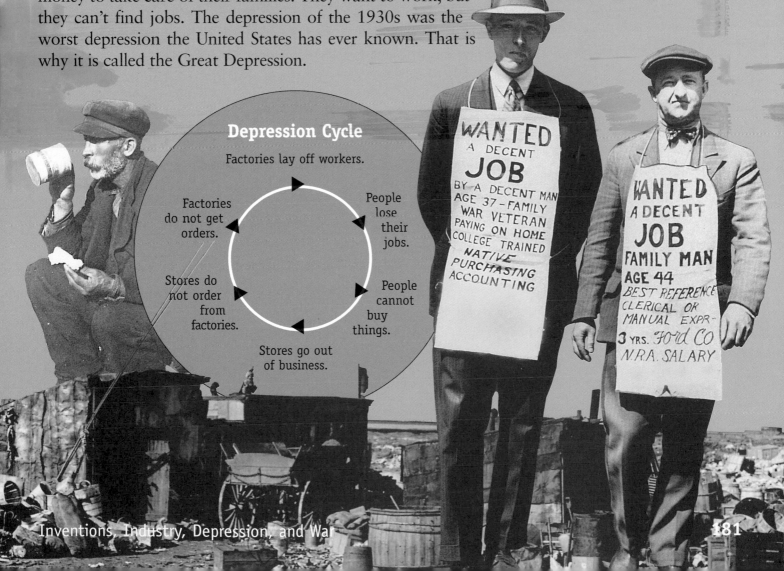

Depression Cycle

Factories lay off workers.

Factories do not get orders.

People lose their jobs.

Stores do not order from factories.

People cannot buy things.

Stores go out of business.

WANTED A DECENT JOB BY A DECENT MAN AGE 37 – FAMILY WAR VETERAN PAYING ON HOME COLLEGE TRAINED NATIVE PURCHASING ACCOUNTING

WANTED A DECENT JOB FAMILY MAN AGE 44 BEST REFERENCE CLERICAL OR MANUAL EXPR– 3 YRS. FORD CO N.R.A. SALARY

> "I did what I had to do. I always seemed to find a way to make things work. We just did what we had to do, just one day at a time."
>
> —a young mother during the depression

During the depression, people waited in bread lines to get free food.
(Photo by Dorothea Lange)

Farmers felt the depression first. After World War I American farmers continued to harvest large crops. With large amounts of farm products, prices went down. Farmers who had borrowed money to buy equipment and seed couldn't pay their bills. Many lost their farms.

Property was very cheap. Many people sold their homes and other property. People stopped buying things such as radios, cars, and washing machines. That left stores with goods they couldn't sell. Factories did not need to produce as much so they sent workers home. Without paychecks, workers couldn't spend as much as they had before. More businesses slowed down. Buying now and paying later soon caught up with people. Businesses could no longer give credit.

Then the stock market crashed. Stock is a small share of a company. People buy and sell stocks. The price of stocks went so low that banks and other people who bought stocks lost large amounts of money. Banks closed because they ran out of money. If anyone had any savings, it was quickly used up to buy food, clothing, or shelter.

Men sold apples on street corners to earn money. People stood in long lines to get free soup and bread. They grew gardens in their backyards. They saved everything they could. They mended old clothes again and again to make them last longer.

In one school, a teacher asked a girl, "What's wrong with you?"

"I'm just hungry," the girl said.

"You may go home and eat," the teacher said.

"I can't," the child answered. "Today is my sister's turn to eat."

People throughout New Jersey tried to help each other as much as they could. Organizations such as the Salvation Army, Red Cross, and many churches and synagogues all pitched in. But life was hard in New Jersey, just like everywhere else. The mills in Paterson shut down. Factories in Camden, Newark, and Passaic closed.

▲ Photo by Dorothea Lange

The New Deal

The government decided to take action. President Franklin Roosevelt wanted people to start working again. He had a plan. He called his plan the New Deal, because it would give Americans a "new deal of the cards." He started projects in order to create jobs. The government hired people to build dams, repair highways, build new courthouses and schools, and fix up parks.

The government loaned farmers money so they could stay in business. Young people were trained for jobs. Children got free school lunches.

One of the new programs was the Civilian Conservation Corps (CCC). The CCC put men to work in state parks across America. The Works Progress Administration (WPA) also started to put people to work on projects that would improve the country. Many of New Jersey's highways, forests, schools, public buildings, and bridges were built or improved because of the new programs.

New welfare programs helped families who needed food, clothing, or a place to live.

Linking the past and the present

Social Security was set up because of the New Deal. If you are an American citizen, you have a Social Security number. Your parents use it on their tax reports. You will use it when you get a job. Memorize your Social Security number.

Work projects in many places gave people jobs.

Americans went to Europe and Asia to fight in World War II.

"Man for man, America's workers and America's soldiers are the best in the world! We helped them build our nation . . . we'll help them defend it."

PRODUCE FOR VICTORY!

Women went to work to help the war effort.

A Second World War

President Roosevelt's New Deal was helping to end the Great Depression. Then something happened that ended the depression for good—a war.

Only twenty years after the end of World War I, fighting broke out again in Europe. Germany, under the leadership of Adolph Hitler and the Nazi Party, invaded Poland. Soon England, France, and Russia were fighting Germany again. They were known as the Allied Powers.

The United States did not get involved for the first two years. It entered the war after a surprise attack on Pearl Harbor, Hawaii. Japanese planes bombed a U.S. naval base there. Nearly 3,000 people were killed or wounded, and many American ships and planes were destroyed. The next day President Roosevelt asked for a declaration of war. The U.S. joined the Allied Powers.

Help from Home

People who stayed at home did their part. Again the factories were turning out war materials. Everyone worked together harder than ever.

Farmers grew extra crops and people bought war bonds. Communities collected rubber tires and other things that could be recycled into equipment that was needed for the war. People who had backyards grew "victory gardens" so they would not have to buy as many fruits and vegetables at the store. This way the farmers would be able to supply more food for the men and women in the armed forces.

It was hard to get such things as sugar, meat, and coffee. Nylon stockings, tires, and alarm clocks were scarce. The materials that went into making those items were being used to make bullets, parachutes, and other war goods. Some goods were sent to the soldiers overseas.

More women began to work at jobs outside the home. Many of them worked at jobs men used to do. People found out that women were good aircraft mechanics, welders, truck drivers, and carpenters.

Some teenagers were allowed to quit school and go to work in factories. Children collected pots, pans, and tin cans that could be turned into metal for making ships.

Rationed Goods

One way to save things that were scarce was to **ration** them. This meant people could buy only so much sugar, meat, butter, coffee, gas, and tires. Each family was given ration stamps every month to buy these things. When their stamps ran out, they could not buy the items until the next month when they would get more stamps.

◀ Ration coupon provided by Beth Gerrard Allen

New Jersey Helps in the Cause

Army camps located at Camp Kilmer and Fort Dix in New Jersey started training thousands of men to be soldiers and pilots. This time a far greater number was called from New Jersey. Over 500,000 served in the armed forces.

World War II put factories back to work. Instead of silk shirts, Paterson factories made army *fatigues*. Shipyards were set up in Camden and Kearny.

These men were prisoners at a concentration camp. Women and children were also sent to the camps.

The Holocaust

Millions of soldiers and civilians died during World War II. That didn't include the death of six million Jews in Europe. They didn't lose their lives by fighting in combat or by living in cities that were bombed. They were murdered. They died for one reason only—because they were Jewish. That mass murder is called the *Holocaust*.

How did that happen? When Adolf Hitler became the leader of Germany, he made one law after another that took rights away from Jewish people. They were forced out of their jobs. Their own country said they were no longer citizens. Many Jews fled Germany, but most stayed. They thought that, as Germans, they would be safe. They were wrong.

Jewish synagogues, where they held religious services, were destroyed. Jews were loaded onto trains. Everything they owned was taken away. Family members were separated. Many never saw each other again.

After rounding up Jews from several European countries, Hitler had them sent to **concentration camps.** The camps were surrounded with barbed wires and armed guards. The people in the camps were forced to do hard labor. At the camps, millions of Jews were killed. Those who weren't killed were treated horribly. Some were even used as slave workers in factories. There was hardly anything to eat and no way to keep warm.

When the war ended, U.S. soldiers went to free the people in the concentration camps. They were shocked and horrified at what they found. The survivors looked like walking skeletons.

The damage to the Jewish people was too enormous ever to be repaired. Entire families were wiped out. Survivors spent a lifetime looking for lost relatives.

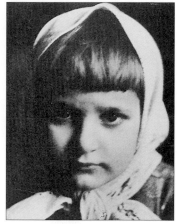

A young Jewish girl wrote: "Next year would have been my last year at school, but I won't be able to graduate . . . the schools have closed. . . . The Nazis have forced more than 5,000 Jews . . . to live in one small area of the town."

Anne Frank

One of the best ways to learn about World War II and the Holocaust is from people who were there. Anne Frank was a Jew who lived in the Netherlands. During the war, her family went into hiding. Unfortunately, Anne Frank did not survive the Holocaust.

Anne received a diary as a present for her thirteenth birthday. In it, she wrote, "Despite all that has happened, I still believe people are good at heart." Anne Frank's words live on. They were published in *Anne Frank: The Diary of a Young Girl.*

Anne Frank wrote on this photo, "This is a photo as I would wish myself to look all the time. Then I would maybe have a chance to come to Hollywood."

To end the war with Japan, the United States dropped atomic bombs on two cities in Japan. Luckily, these terrible weapons have never again been used.

The Atomic Bomb

During the war, countries on both sides tried to build a super bomb. The United States and Great Britain finished the bomb first. They won the race when scientists figured out how to split the *atom*. They could now produce a new form of energy called atomic energy. That energy was used in two bombs that finally ended World War II.

The atom bomb was dropped on Hiroshima and Nagasaki, Japan. It destroyed much of the cities. It killed many people. The United States leaders felt it was important to end the war so more people would not be killed in the fighting. Albert Einstein and Thomas Edison were involved in the science of making the bomb.

An End at Last

In 1945, the war came to an end. Germany, Italy, and Japan surrendered to the United States and the Allies.

New Jerseyans returned home and started to pick up their lives again. Now there were thousands of people looking for jobs and places to live. New challenges faced New Jersey and the entire country.

A Booming State and Nation

Our country was grateful for the sacrifices of all the soldiers, pilots, and others who helped win the war. The government passed a law that would help soldiers who had gone to war pay for their education. It was called the GI Bill. Thousands of ex-soldiers went to colleges and trade schools in New Jersey. They were also able to get loans to buy homes and start businesses.

Searching for the Answers—Your Own Interview

Interview someone who lived during World War II. Choose a grandparent, family friend, or neighbor who lived during World War II.

Before the interview, get together with your class and make a list of questions you would like the person to answer. What kinds of things do you want to know? Here are some suggestions:

- How old were you when the war started?
- What do you remember most about the war?
- How were things different after the war ended?
- How might life be different today if the United States had not fought in the war?

Chapter 11 Review

1. List two inventions of Thomas Edison.
2. How did New Jersey help the country in World War I?
3. How did the Great Depression affect farmers?
4. How did President Roosevelt put people back to work?
5. Why did the United States enter World War II?
6. What was the Holocaust?
7. Name three things made in New Jersey that were used in World War II.

Geography Tie-In

1. The United States fought in World War I and World War II. List the countries or regions against which the United States fought. Find the places on a map of the world.
2. Explain why Hoboken was a good place for soldiers to sail from when they were going to Europe.

THE TIME
1945–2000

PEOPLE TO KNOW
Dr. Martin Luther King Jr.
Kenneth Gibson
Samuel Howard Woodson
Christine Todd Whitman
Norman Schwarzkopf
Alfred Joyce Kilmer
Stephen Crane
Walt Whitman
William Carlos Williams
James Fenimore Cooper
Lillian Gilbreth
Judy Blume
Walter Schirra Jr.
Buzz Aldrin
Carl Lewis
Franco Harris

PLACES TO LOCATE
Rutherford
Montclair
Glen Ridge
Augusta
Willingboro
Mt. Holly
Margate City
Bordentown
Atlantic City

A Time of Growth and Change

1947
New Jersey's third state
constitution is adopted.

1950–1953
Korean War

1960s
Civil Rights Movement

1969
Buzz Aldrin walks on the moon.

1968
Dr. Martin Luther King Jr.
is assassinated.

timeline of events

1945   1950   1955   1960   1965

1950s
The Baby Boomers start families
and move to the suburbs.

1962
Walter Schirra completes
six orbits in space.

1967–1968
Local civil rights
protests turn to riots

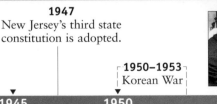

chapter 12

The Jersey City skyline changes with the times. (Photo by Scott Barrow)

TERMS TO UNDERSTAND
segregate
protest
assassinate
tension
challenge
feminist
preservation
crisis
fiction
psychology

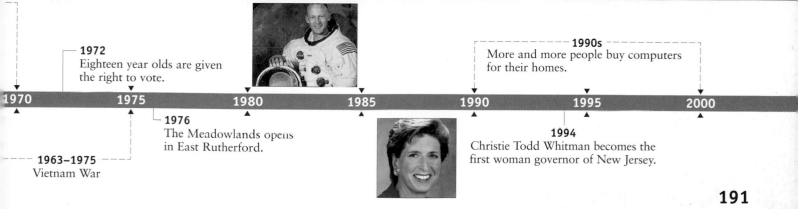

1972
Eighteen year olds are given the right to vote.

1990s
More and more people buy computers for their homes.

1970   1975   1980   1985   1990   1995   2000

1976
The Meadowlands opens in East Rutherford.

1963–1975
Vietnam War

1994
Christie Todd Whitman becomes the first woman governor of New Jersey.

In the 1950s, families watched television for the first time.

In 1958 Hula-Hoops went on sale for the first time. They were a big hit for boys and girls of the 1950s. Kids also roller-skated and rode bicycles around their neighborhoods.

Economic Boom

PEOPLE HAD LITTLE TO SPEND their money on during World War II. Factories were busy making goods to help win the war. That changed when the war ended. Factories started making consumer goods again. They made refrigerators, stoves, washing machines, furniture, televisions, radios, and lawn mowers.

Fast food restaurant chains also started at this time. This meant that companies opened the same kind of restaurant in several cities. People started eating out more often.

People also spent money on music. They bought thousands of phonographs (record players). The most popular music was something new called rock and roll. Everyone wanted records by Bo Diddley, Jerry Lee Lewis, the Supremes, and Elvis Presley.

Baby Boom

The world was at peace and the future seemed safe. There seemed to be jobs for everyone. Families started having more babies. That's why adults born just after the war are called "Baby Boomers."

Larger families bought more goods. They needed clothes, diapers, food, furniture, and bigger houses. They also wanted larger and faster automobiles.

Cars and Roads

Advertisements told families that cars could take people to work and into the country on vacations. The ads also changed people's minds about how many cars one family needed. They said one car was enough for work. But a second car was also necessary, they said, to take children to school and pick up groceries.

With all the new cars came new roads and highways. President Dwight Eisenhower signed a bill that created a new kind of highway. It was called the interstate. Interstate highways connect one state with another. In times of war they would be used to move troops and supplies. At all other times Americans could use the roads for business and recreation.

The Suburbs

Automobiles led to another new invention in the twentieth century—suburbs. Cars and highways let people live in houses farther away from their places of work. They could drive to work, park their cars, and then drive home. The areas that grew up outside the cities, with rows and rows of houses, are called suburbs. Many New Jerseyans live in the suburbs outside of Philadelphia and New York City. All large cities today have suburbs.

Linking the past and the present

Today the interstate highway system is filled with cars, buses, and trucks. Check a New Jersey road map and see how many roads and highways pass through the state.

▶ Photo by Scott Barrow

This highway pattern is called a cloverleaf. Can you tell why?

Civil Rights

In the South, white people made laws that African Americans had to follow. The laws were used to keep white people separate from African Americans. African American students had to attend separate schools. African Americans had to sit in the back of buses. Water fountains had signs above them that said "white only" or "black only." Movie theaters had "colored only" seats. Even many cemeteries were *segregated*.

As time went on, African American leaders had enough. In Alabama, one such leader was Dr. Martin Luther King Jr. People invited King to speak in city after city. He helped them organize peaceful protests. He spoke about the words found in the Declaration of Independence. He reminded the country that

> "Don't let anybody make you feel you are a nobody. If you are ashamed of yourself because you are black, I pity you. I am black, but I'm black and beautiful."
>
> —Martin Luther King Jr.

African Americans were not the only people who were discriminated against. In many places, Hispanic and Chinese people had to sit upstairs in theaters and could not go to skating rinks or bowling alleys.

▲ Photo from New Jersey Newsphotos

Dr. Martin Luther King Jr. greets children during his walking tour of Newark in 1968. He toured the city and saw where much of the violence took place during the riots.

The New Jersey Adventure

"all men are created equal." He led marches to call attention to these issues. The struggle for civil rights was picking up speed. It would continue throughout the rest of the century.

Sadly, Dr. King was *assassinated* in 1968.

Civil Rights in New Jersey

A riot is a terrible thing anytime, anywhere. A riot usually happens when two or more groups cannot solve their differences with words. They turn to violence to try to solve their problems.

In Newark, a problem reached a breaking point when an African American cab driver was pulled over for following a police car too closely. He did not have a driver's license. As a result, the police arrested him. When he arrived at the police station, he either refused or couldn't walk from the police car, so he was dragged into the station. People living in a housing project across the street saw this going on. Soon rumors spread about how the police had handled the problem. Other things happened between the police and the public that led to *tension* and rioting.

During the riots, twenty-six people were killed. Twenty-four of them were African Americans. Because of the rioting, people lost electricity, buses and trains stopped running, and businesses closed. African American leaders asked that the state police and national guard be ordered out of Newark. They felt that the police were creating more tension in the city. Governor Hughes ordered the pull-out of the national guard and state police. Soon, basic services were working again. Electricity came back on, roads were cleared, and businesses re-opened.

Americans with Disabilities Act (ADA)

In 1990, the United States Congress passed a law that protects the rights of all citizens who have physical or mental disabilities. The law says that these people should not be treated unfairly when they apply for a job, use public restrooms, or use any type of transportation. Schools, offices, department stores, supermarkets, theaters, and stadiums must be built so that people who are physically *challenged* can get in and out without too much trouble.

This man is lying down as a peaceful way of protesting.

Kenneth Gibson was the first African American to be elected mayor of Newark.

Samuel Howard Woodson

As an African American member of the New Jersey Assembly, Woodson worked to get more diversity in government. He wanted people with all different backgrounds to work together on things that could change lives for the better. Today he is a retired minister and politician.

New Jersey Portrait

Christie Todd Whitman
1946–
New Jersey's first woman governor, Christie Whitman, was born in New York City. She was raised in Oldwick Township. Governor Whitman attended a private elementary and high school in Far Hills and New York City. As governor, Whitman cut taxes. She also created more jobs. Welfare reform and money for public schools were important. The *preservation* of open space and farmland were also important to Whitman.
While she was governor, President Bush asked Mrs. Whitman to lead an agency that protects the environment of the entire country.

The Women's Movement

Women also fought for equal rights and opportunities during this time. Groups of women joined together to try to make women's wages equal to men's, elect more women to government offices, and give women other rights equal to men. These women were called *feminists*.

Other women, however, did not like the women's movement. They thought that more women going to work would not be good for children and families. They didn't think women should always be treated the same as men.

Women's Rights in New Jersey

1970– U.S. Supreme Court orders a glass company of New Jersey to pay male and female workers the same wage.

1973– The New Jersey chapter of NOW (National Organization of Women) is chartered.

1974– A New Jersey court rules that little league teams have to admit girls.

1982– Marie L. Garibaldi becomes the first woman to serve on the New Jersey Supreme Court.

1983– Barbara Boggs Sigmund becomes the first female mayor of Princeton.

This poster tried to get women to strike for better jobs and equal pay with men.

1992– The New Jersey Supreme Court rules that women can be members of eating clubs at Princeton University.

1993– Princeton professor Toni Morrison becomes the first African American woman to win the Nobel Prize for literature.

More Wars

Since the end of World War II, people from New Jersey have fought in the Korean War, the Vietnam War, the Persian Gulf War, and other wars for short periods of time.

The Vietnam War

For over ten years, the United States was involved in a war between North and South Vietnam. It was our country's longest war. Almost a million people were killed, wounded, or missing in action. More than 212,000 people of New Jersey served in Vietnam.

There were many protests by those who felt that America should not be involved in the war. Finally, the long war was over, and American soldiers came home.

In 1995, Governor Christie Todd Whitman dedicated the New Jersey Vietnam Veterans' Memorial in Holmdel. The names of more than 1,000 servicemen who were killed or missing in action are engraved on the memorial.

Over 20,000 people cheered when General Norman Schwarzkopf, a native of New Jersey who served in Vietnam, said, "Vietnam veterans have every right to be proud of their service to their country!"

Holmdel •

Recent Immigrants

Since the end of World War II, people have kept coming to New Jersey to live. Many immigrants study to become citizens of the United States. They work all day and then go to classes in the evening to learn English. They also learn the American way of life. When they are ready, they take a test. If they pass, they promise to live according to the laws of America and their state. There is usually a ceremony in the county courthouse. It is a very proud moment for the new Americans.

In 2002, New Jersey had over 8 million people. About 55 thousand of them were new immigrants.

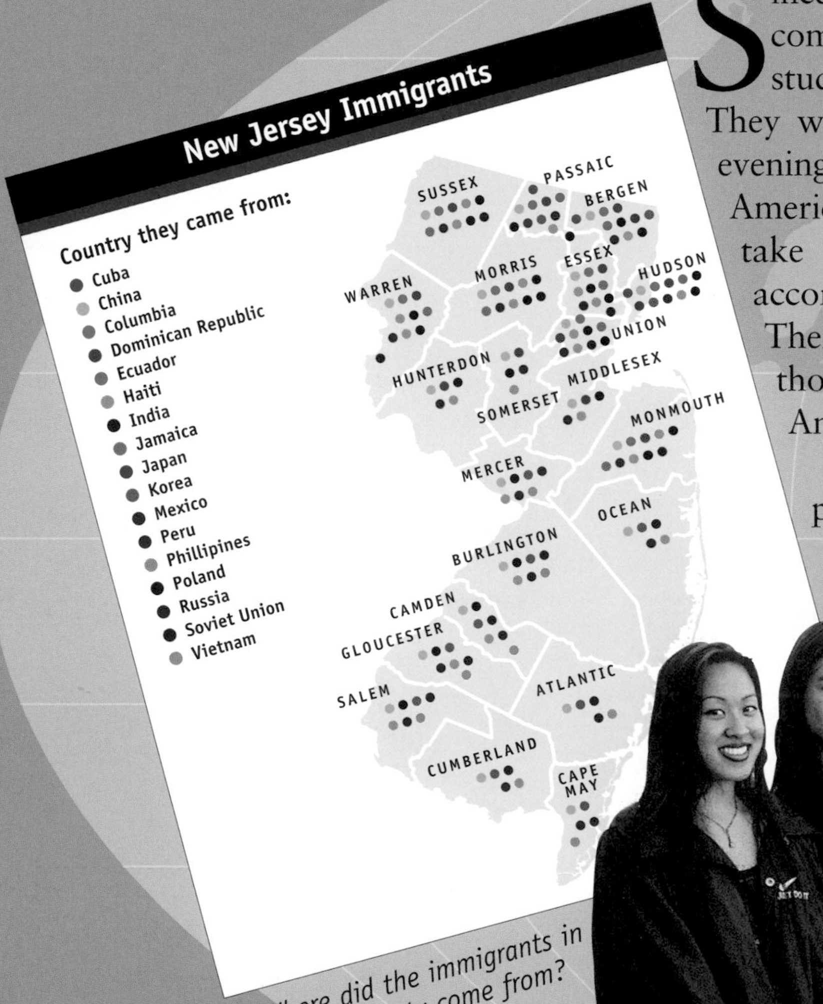

New Jersey Immigrants

Country they came from:

- Cuba
- China
- Columbia
- Dominican Republic
- Ecuador
- Haiti
- India
- Jamaica
- Japan
- Korea
- Mexico
- Peru
- Phillipines
- Poland
- Russia
- Soviet Union
- Vietnam

SUSSEX PASSAIC BERGEN WARREN MORRIS ESSEX HUDSON HUNTERDON UNION SOMERSET MIDDLESEX MERCER MONMOUTH OCEAN BURLINGTON CAMDEN GLOUCESTER ATLANTIC SALEM CUMBERLAND CAPE MAY

Where did the immigrants in your county come from?

New Immigrants, 2000

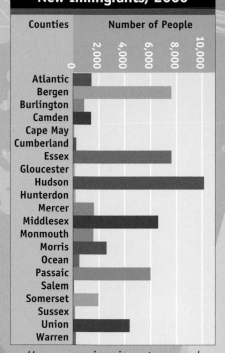

Counties	Number of People
Atlantic	
Bergen	
Burlington	
Camden	
Cape May	
Cumberland	
Essex	
Gloucester	
Hudson	
Hunterdon	
Mercer	
Middlesex	
Monmouth	
Morris	
Ocean	
Passaic	
Salem	
Somerset	
Sussex	
Union	
Warren	

How many immigrants moved to your county?

From Fort to Village

People come to America for many reasons. One reason is because there is a war in their country. This is true of immigrants from Kosovo. They left Kosovo, in the southern part of Yugoslavia, and came to Fort Dix in New Jersey. Refugees, forced from their homes, left Kosovo by the thousands. The families traveled mostly by foot. They were weak and hungry. Many had lost loved ones because of the war. Others were separated from their families.

Some refugees were brought to Fort Dix for background checks and medical examinations. They started calling the fort a "village." The Fort Dix cooks learned how to prepare food from Kosovo. For the refugees at Fort Dix, many things in life were hard. They were unsure if they would go back to their homeland or stay in the United States.

For one baby, becoming an American was easy. After his parents fled Kosovo, a baby boy was born in New Jersey. His parents named him "Amerikan."

At Fort Dix, the refugees got flip flops to wear on their feet in the shower. But they started to wear them everywhere, even with suits and ties. The flip flops became a symbol for their new American experience.

Lebibe Karaliju, a Kosovo refugee, holds baby Amerikan.

Bringing Words to Life

NEW JERSEY WRITERS have reached people all around the world. Writers take us to exciting places. We don't even have to leave our home!

(Alfred) Joyce Kilmer
(1886–1918)

"I think that I shall never see, a poem as lovely as a tree" are the opening lines of Joyce Kilmer's poem, *Trees*.

Born in New Brunswick, Kilmer was one of America's finest poets. He worked as an editor for newspapers. When World War I started, he joined the army and was killed during a battle in France.

Stephen Crane
(1871–1900)

Stephen Crane was born in Newark. He was one of America's great writers. Crane's stories seem very real even though they are *fiction*. He spent most of his early years in New York. After graduating from college, he moved to New York City. He struggled there as a writer.

His most famous novel is *The Red Badge of Courage*. This is a story about a young Union soldier who becomes a hero during the Civil War.

Stephen Crane

▲ Illustrations from North Wind ▶

◀ *Walt Whitman*

Walt Whitman
(1819–1892)

Walt Whitman is one of America's finest poets. He wrote about the importance of each person. Whitman lived in Camden. Many writers and artists visited him. In Camden, he wrote many of his finest poems. One of his most famous poems is "Song of Myself."

William Carlos Williams

(1883–1963)

Williams was a doctor and a poet. He lived in Rutherford. His masterpiece is *Paterson*, a long poem. The poem tells the story of the Great Falls from wilderness to big city.

James Fenimore Cooper

(1789–1851)

James Fenimore Cooper, one of America's finest writers, was born in Burlington. The beautiful area of upper New York State, with all its beauty, inspired most of his written works. At age thirteen, Cooper attended Yale University for three years. Later he went to sea and served in the navy. Then Cooper got married and became a farmer.

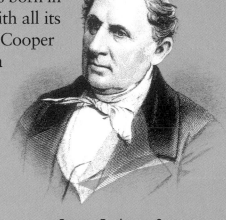

James Fenimore Cooper

One of his most famous publications was a group of stories called the *Leatherstocking Tales*. There were five novels in the series. The most famous ones are *The Last of the Mohicans* and *The Deerslayer*.

Lillian Gilbreth

(1878–1972)

Lillian Gilbreth was from Montclair. She was known throughout the world for her strong feelings about people being more important than machines. *Psychology* is the science that studies how the mind works and how humans or animals behave. This was the lifetime work of Gilbreth. She was the mother of twelve children. You can read about her very interesting life in the funny book, *Cheaper by the Dozen*.

Judy Blume

(1938–   )

Judy Blume was born in Elizabeth. Her books may be funny sometimes, but they really tell about the feelings of young people like you. Some of her most popular stories are: *Super Fudge*, *Then Again, Maybe I Won't*, and *Otherwise Known as Sheila the Great*. Over sixty-five million copies of her books have been sold. Blume's books are sold in twenty languages.

Judy Blume ▶

Photo by Peter Simon

A Time of Growth and Change

201

New Jersey in Space

When most people hear the word "pioneer," they think of someone moving out west in a covered wagon. Today, we still have pioneers. Instead of wagons, they're travelling in spaceships.

Wally Schirra Jr. was born in Hackensack. He was a graduate of the United States Naval Academy and in 1959 he was selected as one of the seven *Mercury* astronauts. He took part in three space flights for a total of twelve days. Shirra was the commander of the backup crew for the *Apollo 1* mission. The first meeting between two orbiting spacecraft took place in 1965. Schirra and another pilot guided *Gemini* 6 to within a foot of *Gemini* 7.

"Buzz" Aldrin was born in Glen Ridge. He went to the United States Military Academy and the Massachusetts Institute of Technology. On July 20, 1969, he became the second human being to set foot on the moon. For two hours he and Neil Armstrong collected moon rocks. They brought back many samples to Earth for scientific study.

Wally Schirra Jr. was an astronaut from New Jersey.

"Buzz" Aldrin walked on the moon.

Sports

All kinds of sports and activities take place in New Jersey. People play sports professionally and for fun. What sports do you like the best?

Carl Lewis

Carl Lewis is one of the greatest track stars ever. Although Lewis was born in Alabama, his family moved to Willingboro two years later. His mother and father became track coaches at the local high school. His brother and sister were also terrific athletes.

When he was eight, Carl was part of his parents' track club. Before anyone knew it, he grew up to be one of the greatest track athletes Willingboro High School ever had.

In 1984 Lewis entered his first Olympic Games and won four gold medals. In 1988, he won two more, and in 1992 he walked away with two more. He entered his last Olympic Games in 1996. He was thirty-six years old then, and ended up winning a ninth gold medal in the long jump. He broke the world record for the long jump.

Franco Harris

Another great athlete from New Jersey is football player Franco Harris. Harris was born in Mt. Holly. Today he calls New York City his home. Harris was a high school All-American at Rancocas Valley Regional School in Mt. Holly. He went to Penn State University. He then became a running back for the Pittsburgh Steelers. In 1975, he was named Super Bowl Most Valuable Player. He was 6'2," weighed 230, and played as number 32. In 1990, Harris was voted into the Football Hall of Fame. Following his football career, he appeared in a few television programs.

The New Jersey Cardinals are the farm team for the St. Louis Cardinals. They play in Augusta.

Carl Lewis

New Jersey Legends

Lucy the Elephant

James V. Lafferty wanted something very special to attract people to South Atlantic City. He came up with the idea of building a giant elephant. Her name is Lucy.

Lucy the elephant was once a home. In 1902, a doctor from England built a four-room apartment inside her for himself and his family. They stayed there during their summers at the Jersey Shore.

After many years, Lucy got old. She needed to be fixed up. Although many people wanted to see Lucy torn down and taken away, she still stands today on the shore of Margate City.

There She Is

It all started in 1921 and it is still known today as the Miss America Beauty Pageant. Millions of people throughout the world watch the pageant on television. The contest was held in Atlantic City for more than 80 years. It offers one of the richest scholarships available for women.

Margate City Atlantic City

How Big Is Lucy?

Imagine legs that are 10 feet across and 22 feet high. The body is 38 feet long and 80 feet around. The head is 26 feet long and 58 feet around. Now an elephant must have a tail, but a 26-foot long one? We can't forget a trunk. It must be some job to swing a 36-foot one. Last but not least, Lucy has two huge 22-foot tusks.

Try to measure Lucy's size on your school playground.

The New Jersey Adventure

September 11, 2001

On the morning of September 11, 2001, New York City's World Trade Center towers were destroyed by foreign terrorists. The terrorists had boarded airplanes and took over the planes from their pilots. The terrorists flew the planes to New York City.

The first plane crashed into the upper floors of the North Tower. Usually 50,000 people would have been working there, but many people were still on their way to work and had not arrived at their offices yet. Soon, a second plane crashed into the South Tower. This plane caused an explosion, a huge fire, and the building started to crash to the ground. Soon, both towers were completely gone. The rubble buried people who worked in the buildings and firefighters who had come to help.

Hundreds of New Jersey people saw this terrible event as they stood on the opposite shore of the Hudson River. Many people from New Jersey were employed at the World Trade Center.

Two other planes had also been taken over by terrorists. One flew into the Pentagon in Washington, D.C. Another plane crashed in Pennsylvania. Thousands of Americans were killed by the four crashes. All over America and in other countries, people gathered in parks and churches, along shorelines and streets, and shared their anger and sorrow. "How could strangers do these terrible things to America?" they asked. In every city, people hung American flags on their porches and in front of buildings.

The first war of the twenty-first century began when President Bush and Congress declared war on terrorism.

To show America's desire for peace after the attack, one group of over a thousand people raised red, white, and blue paper to form a huge flag. Then white doves, symbols of peace, were released to fly over the bright flag and into the blue sky.

What do you think?

Do you remember September 11? What do you remember about it? How did you feel?

A Time of Growth and Change

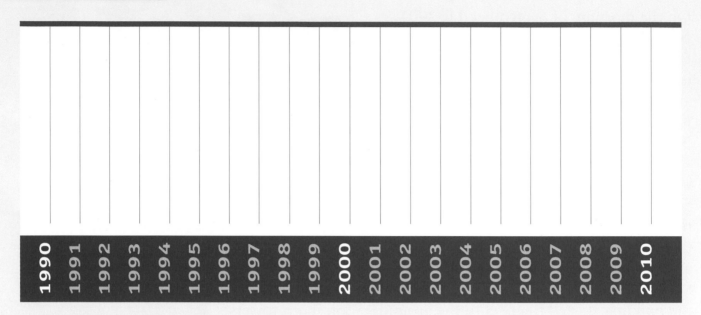

1990 1991 1992 1993 1994 1995 1996 1997 1998 1999 **2000** 2001 2002 2003 2004 2005 2006 2007 2008 2009 **2010**

Personal Histories

The New Jersey Adventure is full of stories of people who make New Jersey what it is today. We know about a lot of these people and the things they did because there are written records of them.

Begin writing your history by making a timeline of your life. Start with today and work backward. Record what you can remember about each year in your life back to your first memory. Then ask your parents to give you information for the early years that you can't remember.

It might help to make a list first. Include:

- The places where your family lived.
- The schools you attended.
- The happiest times and the saddest.
- World events you remember.
- Your favorite music.
- Your favorite games.

Make another list of the people in your life.

- Who is your family?
- Where did they come from?
- Who were your friends?
- Which adults were important to you?
- Who has influenced your life?
- Who were your favorite teachers?

Chapter 12 Review

1. How did the automobile help people move to the suburbs?

2. What are civil rights? Give two examples of groups fighting for civil rights during this time period.

3. What does ADA stand for? How does it protect and help citizens?

4. Describe some of the problems of the Kosovo refugees.

5. In what part of New Jersey are most of the newly arrived immigrants living? Can you explain why?

6. Name three writers from New Jersey. What did each write?

7. Name two things Franco Harris and Carl Lewis have in common.

8. Explain what happened on September 11, 2001.

Geography Tie-In

1. Locate North and South Korea, Vietnam, and the Persian Gulf on a world map. On which continents are these places located?

2. Using the immigration map of New Jersey on page 198, name the countries that immigrants came from. Which oceans did the people from these countries cross to get to the United States?

3. If you were living 200 years ago, before there were any airplanes, which of the countries above would you be able to visit by sailing ship?

4. New Jersey has many important military sites where work is done to support our country's armed forces. On the map on page 117, locate these counties where our government does research, holds supplies, designs aircraft equipment, refuels planes, and trains soldiers. Find Morris, Monmouth, Burlington, and Ocean Counties on the map.

THE TIME
1950–2000

PLACES TO LOCATE
Hackensack
Paterson
Broadway
Roadstown
New Brunswick
Murray Hill
Perth Amboy
Atlantic City
Morristown
Camden
Deepwater
Montvale
Bridgeton
Greenwich
Seaville
Bayonne
West New York

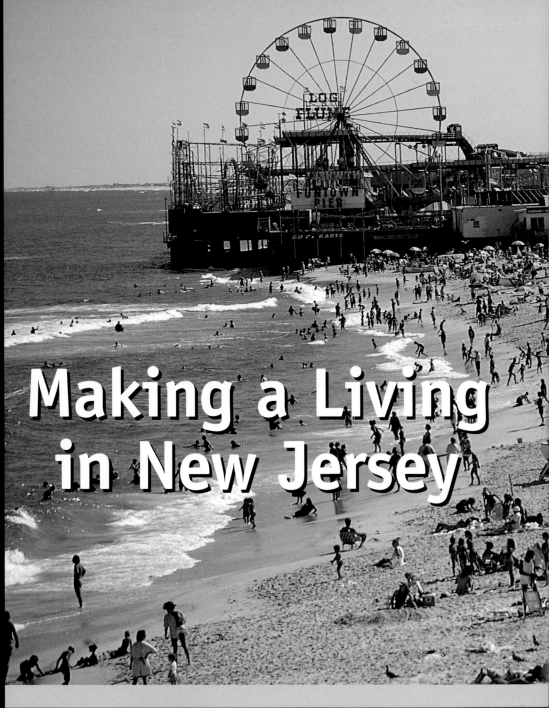

Making a Living in New Jersey

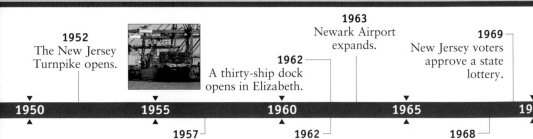

timeline of events

1952
The New Jersey
Turnpike opens.

1962
A thirty-ship dock
opens in Elizabeth.

1963
Newark Airport
expands.

1969
New Jersey voters
approve a state
lottery.

| 1950 | 1955 | 1960 | 1965 | 1970 |

1957
The Garden State
Parkway opens.

1962
Bell Laboratories
launches the
Telstar I satellite.

1968
Garden State Arts Center
(now PNC Bank Arts
Center) opens.

TERMS TO UNDERSTAND
good
service
employee
salary
expense
profit
entrepreneur
foundry
warping
migrant
cultivate
research
corporation
condense
transistor
monopoly
toxic
acid rain

Tourists from all over come to the Jersey Shore. Tourism is important to New Jersey's economy. (Photo by Scott Barrow)

1978
The first legalized gambling casinos open in Atlantic City.

1990
New Jersey's population reaches almost 8 million.

1975 — 1980 — 1985 — 1990 — 1995 — 2000

1976
The Meadowlands Sports Complex opens in East Rutherford.

1980
Newark Airport is rated one of the world's busiest airports.

1993
Liberty Science Center opens at Liberty State Park.

Economics for Everyone

PEOPLE HAVE NEEDS. They also have wants. They need food, clothing, and shelter. They want things like cars, books, toys, and bicycles. These are called *goods*.

People also need care from doctors. They need education from teachers. They may want help repairing their car. These are called *services*.

Economics is the study of how people get the goods and services they need and want. There are many different economic systems in the world. The United States has what is called a free enterprise system. People own the factories and companies that produce goods and services. A business is owned by one or more people. Owners decide what to produce and how much to charge for it. They are in charge of selling the product, too.

Earning Money

Business owners usually hire other people, called *employees*, to work for them. The owner pays the employees a *salary*. Often the employees with the most education and who produce more goods and services earn the most money.

Making a Profit

How do business owners make money? Usually they sell what the workers produce. They can sell goods or services.

Activity

Workplace Skills

Employers expect their employees to be:

- On time
- Hard-working
- Courteous
- Cooperative
- Problem solvers

You can prepare to be a good employee by practicing these skills at school.

Write a sentence about each skill. Explain how you do these things today. Which skills do you want to improve on?

Expense $15
The business pays for the cloth and the zipper. They also pay an employee to make the coat. These are expenses.

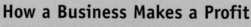

How a Business Makes a Profit

PRICE $45
The business sells the coat for more money than it costs to make it.

PRICE - EXPENSE = PROFIT
$45- $15 = $30
Profit is the money the business earns after all expenses are paid.

Supply and Demand

How do business owners decide how much to charge for their products? The selling price depends on a lot of things. The price has to be more than what it cost the company to make the item, so the business will make a profit. Sometimes the price also depends on how much of something there is. If there are not enough copies of a certain video game for everyone who wants it, the company can sell it for a higher price. People will be willing to pay more to get it. This is called the rule of supply and demand.

Sometimes a company lowers its prices. Maybe a company makes computers, but people don't buy very many of them, so the company has extra computers sitting around. They might lower the price to get people to buy them. A company may come out with a new model of a computer. Then prices would drop on older models.

Scarcity

When things or resources are scarce, there is not enough of them. People, businesses, and even the government has to make choices when things they need are scarce. Should they pay more? Should they buy something else instead?

Economics in Early New Jersey

Today, New Jersey uses the free enterprise system like everywhere else in the United States. However, a system of free enterprise did not always exist here.

The Lenape Indians felt that no one had the right to own land. The land and everything on it was to be shared by everyone.

When fur traders came to Amcrica, they used the beaver fur to make themselves very rich. Even though they did not own the land or beavers, they took it.

Then early settlers started buying and selling goods such as flour, corn, and household items. Stores opened up in towns all across the colonies. Soon money was important. The economy changed.

This man is providing both goods and services. The lobsters are goods. Fishing and preparing the lobsters for sale are services.

When there is a large supply of something, the cost is lower. When there is a small supply of something, the cost is higher. For example, if a store has too many basketballs, the balls might go on sale.

Making a Living in New Jersey

Choosing What to Buy

If you wanted a new bike, how would you choose which one to buy? There are many kinds to choose from. Comparing products is an important part of choosing how to spend money.

First you have to figure out what you need. Do you need a road bike or a mountain bike? You also want to think about what you like. Do you like the green bike or the red one? Then you search for bikes at different stores. You can make a chart to compare the bikes. Then you can choose the bike that fits your needs and wants and has the best price.

Look at this chart. Decide what kind of bike you would buy.

Activity

Make a Product Chart

Think of something you want to buy. Find out as much as you can about the product. Make your own chart to compare the products. Does a chart help you decide how to make the best choice?

Brand	Price	Color	Extras
Brand A	$80	blue	bell
Brand B	$75	red	basket, bell, water bottle
Brand C	$100	silver	flashing lights, 10 speeds, water bottle

Saving and Planning

Money is important to people. It helps them get the things they need and want. Money also gives us a way to plan ahead for things we will want later. Suppose you get an allowance from your family. Or, you might walk dogs or mow lawns. Suppose you earn $10 each week, and you want to buy a scooter that costs $100.

You could save your money until you have enough for the scooter.
- How long would it take if you saved all of the $10 each week?
- How long would it take if you saved $5 and spent $5 each week?

You could save your money in a bank. Banks help people manage their money. They are safe places to keep savings. Banks also make loans. People can go to a bank to borrow money so they can buy a house or a car.

Factors of Production

There are four things that must come together before something is sold as a good or service. These things are called factors of production. Factors of production are land, labor, capital goods, and entrepreneurship. Let's learn what these things mean:

Land (natural resources)
People use the term "land" to mean anything that is found in nature. If you are making chairs, you might use wood. If you are making teddy bears and need cotton to stuff them, you use cotton. Cotton and wood are both natural resources that grow on the land.

Capital Goods
When you use something that is already made to make something else, you are using a capital good. The hammer and nails a carpenter uses are capital goods. The paint, canvas, and brushes an artist uses are capital goods. In business, the money you need to run the business is also called capital.

Labor
To provide goods and services, there must be labor. Labor is the work that people do. Even if you bought a robot, it took labor to make it. Someone built it and someone sold it. Carpenters, teachers, sales people, lawyers, secretaries, actors, racecar drivers, and basketball players all do labor.

Entrepreneurship
Entrepreneurship is owning and running a business. It often starts with an idea. The person must be willing to take a risk to make the idea work. Entrepreneurs use land, labor, and capital goods to make money.

labor is the people working

the natural resource is cotton

capital goods are machines and tools

the entrepreneur is the owner

For a teddy bear factory, the natural resource would be cotton, the labor is the people working, the capital goods are the machines and tools, and the entrepreneur is the owner who came up with the business idea.

John Kyriakopoulos is an entrepreneur who started Daddy's Restaurant in Hackensack. Here is his story in his own words:

"I came to America [from Greece] thirty years ago and I have been working very hard during all that time in different restaurants. But my goal was to have my own place. Two years after I came to the states I opened my first store. It was a Greek-American deli. . . . Business was going very good and in three years I opened four more stores in different towns in New Jersey. All the stores are still doing business. . . . In 1986, I opened the restaurant I still own. Its name is Daddy's and it serves breakfast, lunch, and dinner.

"I never felt sorry that I came to America. My dream came true here. This was possible only in America, the best country in the world, especially the state of New Jersey, which I truly love."

Immigrants Become Entrepreneurs

When immigrants came to this country, most of them got jobs working for other people. The pay was usually very low. If they did not know the language, the men and women had to do jobs that no one else wanted. It was a hard way to live.

People wanted better work. Thousands of immigrants became **entrepreneurs**. An entrepreneur is someone who has an idea and the courage to start a business. Entrepreneurs work for themselves. Usually the whole family helped with the business. Even the children sanded, sewed, hammered, chopped, ran errands, or did whatever needed to be done. When the business grew, the family hired other employees.

Some entrepreneurs sold goods. Maybe they made hats, rugs, tables, or wagons. Maybe they farmed and sold the extra wheat, potatoes, or apples. Maybe they invented a new product and sold it.

Some entrepreneurs sold services. They may have delivered groceries, painted homes, or taught classes. They may have opened their own barbershops and cut hair.

New Jersey Entrepreneurs

Lonnie Stephenson

Lonnie was born in North Carolina in 1930. He did not want to work on the family farm. Instead, he went to Paterson to work at a *foundry*. Lonnie worked there for two hours and quit. He said, "It was worse than the farm."

Within the next year, he found a job as a floor boy in a *warping* mill. He taught himself the process and eventually became a warper. Jobs in the silk industry were usually closed to African Americans, but Lonnie was able to succeed. After three years, the company moved to Broadway and Lonnie was made a supervisor of more than twenty people. He eventually bought the mill. Business has slowed down recently, but he still owns the mill and employs six people.

"When I took over the mill there was a lot of negative talk. I proved I could do it and that I had something to offer."

Todd Henri Daigneault

Todd Daigneault is now known as Chef Todd. After a career as a chef, he started his own business. Here is his story in his own words:

> *Christmas was soon upon us. . . . There wasn't any money . . . for presents to give to family and friends. . . . It was our French custom to give homemade gifts. Our grandparents used to make gifts according to their vocations [jobs]. My grandfather was a lumberjack . . . and he used to make gifts out of wood such as toy trucks and dolls. . . . My grandmother was a seamstress and would make knitted hats, mittens, and quilts. . . . I thought as a chef, maybe I could do the same. So I started to make special blends of herbs, oils, and vinegars to give as gifts. . . . It caught on . . . and before you knew it we were producing different flavors.*
>
> *By listening to people's needs and ideas, our company grew into the Dutch Hill Distillery. Dutch Hill Distillery is now producing dressings and spice blends that are sold on the Internet.*

This man grows and picks beans on a farm in Roadstown.

Photo by Scott Barrow

Making a Living Today

When New Jersey first became a state, almost everyone farmed. Farming is still very important here. But, today most people work in either manufacturing or service jobs. As cities have become larger, the farms have slowly been replaced by the business world of the city.

What do you think?

Do you think there should be a return to the agricultural lifestyle that existed when our state was young? What advantages or disadvantages might there be to a more rural (farm) lifestyle?

Off to the Farm

If you were a farmer in the days of George Washington, most of your tools would have been made from wood and iron. You would plant the same crops year after year on the same ground. You might have to move because all the minerals in the soil were used up and your crops won't grow anymore.

Today, a farmer has a better understanding of the soil. He uses science to help him plant, grow, and harvest his crops. It's not unusual to see the latest computer systems being used on farms. Many farmers use **migrant** workers to help plant, **cultivate,** and harvest crops. Today, machines are replacing many of these workers.

In 1920 there were over 30,000 farmers in New Jersey. Today there are about 8,000. Why do you think the number of farmers has dropped?

The Garden State

Here is a chart that will help you locate each county and some of the products that are either grown or raised there. Research each county to see how many more products you could add to the chart.

County	Farm Product Grown or Raised
Atlantic	blueberries, sweet potatoes
Burlington	apples, blueberries, thoroughbred horses, dairy cows
Cumberland	apples, white potatoes, sweet potatoes, peaches
Gloucester	asparagus, apples, peaches
Hunterdon	eggs, dairy cows
Mercer	white potatoes
Middlesex	white potatoes
Monmouth	white potatoes, thoroughbred horses, ponies, apples
Salem	white potatoes, asparagus, dairy cows
Somerset	thoroughbred horses, ponies

New Jersey, the Little Giant

It all started in Paterson with a few cotton mills. Then New Jersey leaped into the twentieth century as one of the leading manufacturing states in the country. In fact, it is one of the top seven states when it comes to products made in factories.

When it comes to chemicals, New Jersey is number one. Other products include textiles, clothing, food, glass, leather, books, newspapers, and magazines. Engineers and scientists design many products. People are always **researching** new and better ways to produce things.

Large companies called **corporations** have made New Jersey their home. Insurance companies, banks, computer manufacturers, supermarkets, and soup companies are just a few of the hundreds in the state.

Making a Living in New Jersey

New Jersey Companies

Johnson & Johnson

Johnson & Johnson was founded in New Brunswick in the late 1800s. Today it is the world's largest manufacturer of health care products. Its head office is still in New Brunswick. Johnson & Johnson owns companies in Canada, Latin America, Europe, Asia, and Australia. Its products are sold in more than 175 countries. It employs over 90,000 people. Some of its most popular products are Johnson's Baby Powder, Band-Aid Bandages, and Tylenol. Have you used any of these products?

Bristol-Myers Squibb Company

What company makes medicine to make you well and vitamins to keep you healthy? What company makes soap and lotions to keep your hair and skin clean and beautiful? What company employs thousands of New Jersey workers and has offices in sixty other countries?

Bristol-Myers Squibb is one of New Jersey's important companies.

PSE&G

Public Service Enterprise Group (PSE&G) has its head office in Newark. This company owns gas, electric, and transportation companies. Early in this century, PSE&G was involved in trolley and ferry transportation. Then it ran a very large bus service. Over 11,000 people work for the company, and most of them are in New Jersey.

New Jersey Firsts

- Robert W. Johnson and George Seabury made the first Band-Aid bandage in 1870.

- Joseph Campbell started the Campbell Soup Company and made the very first **condensed** soup in the country in 1897.

- Willis Havil and Carrier invented the first room air conditioner in 1911.

- Seabrook Farms produced the first frozen food in 1933.

- Three scientists for the Bell Laboratories in Murray Hill invented the **transistor** in 1947. This led to the invention of the computer chip.

- A factory in Perth Amboy produced the first plastic in the United States.

Enjoy New Jersey!

When people visit New Jersey from other states and countries, they may eat at a restaurant in Paterson, visit Atlantic City, visit the Morristown National Historic Park in Morristown, or go to the New Jersey State Aquarium in Camden. This is all part of a major industry in New Jersey: tourism.

Tourism provides jobs and money because people come to New Jersey and spend money on transportation, lodging, food, entertainment, and recreation. All the things tourists do in our state make money for the businesses and workers of New Jersey.

Atlantic City

Atlantic City is one of the most popular tourist destinations in the world. Over thirty million people visit Atlantic City each year. Many tourists come to gamble at the casinos.

Many new jobs were created when the casinos opened, but there was also an increase in crime. A new public safety building was built in the city. This has helped to lower the crime rate.

Besides gambling, tourists come to visit the boardwalk. The six-mile boardwalk has entertainers, shops, and beaches. There are shops with glass, furniture, paint, boats, and hosiery. There are also terrific swimming and fishing places and great shopping malls. You can buy an Atlantic City invention along the boardwalk—salt water taffy.

Tourists enjoy the aquarium in Camden.

The board game *Monopoly* was invented in Atlantic City in 1930.
In business a **monopoly** happens when one company owns or controls something.

The beaches of Atlantic City are fun places for kids to play.

Transportation

T ransportation of natural resources and finished products is very important for business. Without good transportation, business would almost stop.

Airports

There are 250 airports and over 400 helicopter landing areas in New Jersey. People traveling on business and vacation use them. Police and fire departments and government agencies use them.

Railroads

Railroads have always been an important part of New Jersey's transportation. John Stevens's little steam wagon was just the beginning. Soon many people realized that it would be much easier to use trains to move goods.

Today a Metroliner train can make the trip across the state from Newark to Trenton in less than forty minutes. That's traveling almost over one mile per minute.

Roads and Highways

There are over 30,000 miles of highway which lead in, out, and around the state of New Jersey. Three toll roads can be found there: the New Jersey Turnpike, the Garden State Parkway, and the Atlantic City Expressway.

The New Jersey Turnpike is the busiest toll road in the United States. Traveling from New York State to Cape May we find the Garden State Parkway. One year, over four million vehicles passed through the tollbooths on their way to the Jersey Shore.

Have you ever taken a train trip? Where did you go?

The New Jersey Turnpike is the most used road in the Western Hemisphere.

▲ Photo by Scott Barrow

▲ Photo by Walter Choroszewski

The Atlantic City Expressway leads to many historic sites in the southern part of the state. One can travel on it to see the New Jersey Liberty Bell in Bridgeton; Greenwich, where Patriots burned the British tea; Walt Whitman's home in Camden; and the Friends (Quaker) Meeting House in Seaville.

Look at a road map of the United States. Which two states are difficult or impossible to drive to from New Jersey?

Cargo is loaded and unloaded at Port Elizabeth.

Shipping

New Jersey's location along the water makes it an ideal place for shipping. There are many major ports in New Jersey where goods can be brought in and shipped out. There are about one hundred piers that run along the Hudson River. Cargo is brought in and out from the piers. Major ports are located in Newark, Elizabeth, and Raritan.

The Port of Newark is one of the busiest ports in the world. Docks and piers have been built along the bay. Railroads have run their tracks right up to the end of the piers. Ships can now be loaded and unloaded at dockside.

Jersey City is also a seaport city. Just like in Newark, railroad companies brought their tracks into the city and close to the docks. From Hoboken, ocean liners dock and sail for ports all over the world. The dock at Bayonne ships a lot of oil.

Pollution and the Environment

Water

Everyone needs water for drinking and washing. Plants need water, too. Can you think of more ways in which water is used?

Factories have to be very careful to not spill any *toxic* waste into the rivers and oceans. Would anyone be able to eat anything that came from polluted water? Imagine swimming in the ocean with garbage floating around you. Our state and federal governments have very strict laws against pollution of any kind.

Air

Can factories pollute the air? What parts of New Jersey do you think will have the highest levels of air pollution? If factories send toxic gasses into the air, the clouds can become full of harmful chemicals. Raindrops carry these harmful chemicals into the soil and water.

Look up at the clouds. Do they stay still or do they move? Many times the polluted rain, called *acid rain*, falls in places far away from the factories. This acid rain can harm the life in the rivers, lakes, and ponds. Today there are laws against polluting the air. Factories try to keep the air clean.

Soil

The soil can become just as polluted as the air and water. When garbage is left on the ground, much of it can slowly seep into the soil. Many large cities truck their garbage to places called landfills. "Landfill" means exactly what it says. Deep, long ditches are dug far away from any natural water sources and the garbage is dumped into them. The land is filled up with the garbage. Is there any way the garbage can be used to help people? Someone came up with the idea of burning it to create electrical energy that could be used by homes, factories, and hospitals.

Metal is recycled in New Jersey.

Photo by Scott Barrow

> **What do you think?**
>
> **Why do you think the landfills are far away from natural water sources such as rivers, oceans, lakes, and ponds?**

Goods and Services

Goods are things that are usually manufactured. This means they are made in factories, workshops, or even at home. They are then sold for money. Shoes, pencils, televisions, and dog collars are all goods. People make money by making and selling goods.

Services are things that people do for other people. Dentists, sales clerks, umpires, coaches, and your teacher are providing services. People earn money by providing services.

Don't be fooled! Many people who provide a service also use goods. The sales clerk, for example, is providing a service by selling shoes. The shoes are goods, but the sales clerk provides a service by selling them to you.

On a separate piece of paper, number from one to thirteen. Write **G** for goods or **S** for services for each job listed below.

1. Works with plumbing
2. Collects the garbage
3. Teaches students
4. Manufactures paint
5. Paints pictures to sell
6. Makes engines for cars
7. Repairs cars
8. Wraps cheese in a factory
9. Delivers cheese to grocery stores
10. Makes telephones
11. Repairs telephones
12. Manufactures light bulbs
13. What you would like to do when you grow up

Chapter 13 Review

1. What is the difference between a good and a service?
2. Briefly explain how a capitalistic system works.
3. List the four factors of production. Give an example of each.
4. How did children of immigrant entrepreneurs help their parents?
5. What expenses might be involved in starting up a business?
6. How do modern farmers use technology?
7. Name two corporations located in New Jersey.
8. Name two places in New Jersey that are popular with tourists.
9. Why is shipping in New Jersey so important to the state? Why is it important to the rest of the world?

Geography Tie-In

1. What geographical features make New Jersey a popular place for tourists?
2. What geographical features make New Jersey a good place for shipping?

GLOSSARY

The terms are identified according to their use in the chapters of this textbook.

abolitionist: a person who wanted to end slavery

acid rain: rain that contains harmful chemicals

ally: a group working with another group for a common cause

amendment: a change made to the U.S. Constitution

amphibian: animals that live in both land and water, such as frogs and toads

anchor: to hold in place with an anchor or heavy weight

apprentice: a person learning a craft from a skilled worker

archaeologist: a scientist who learns about ancient people by studying the things they left behind

artifact: an object made by people long ago

assassinate: to murder by sudden or secret attack

assembly: a group of law makers

asylum: a place where needy, sick, or mentally ill people can receive care

atom: a tiny particle that can produce nuclear energy

auction: a sale in which the items are sold to the highest bidder

average: the mean between the highest and lowest; a typical amount

barge: a wide flat-bottomed boat

barracks: a building or group of buildings where soldiers live

barter: to trade one thing for another without the use of money

bill: a written idea for a law

brigade: a large group of soldiers

canal: a waterway made by people rather than by nature

capitalist: where people, not the government, own the land and wealth, and businesses compete with each other to make a profit

caravan: a group of travelers journeying together

challenge: something difficult that must be overcome

circa: about, approximately

civil rights: the rights that belong to every citizen

civilian: a citizen who is not in the army

clan: a group of families with a common ancestor

colonist: someone who settles in a new country

colony: a territory under the control of another nation

committee: a group of people who meet to talk about certain things

communist: when the government owns the means of production instead of the people

compromise: to give up something you want in order to reach an agreement with someone

concentration camp: a type of camp where Jewish prisoners were kept, tortured, and killed during World War II

condense: to make more compact

conflict: a disagreement or struggle

conserve: to keep in good condition; to keep from losing or wasting

consumer: a person who buys things, a person who spends money

continent: one of the seven large land areas of the world

corporation: a large company

country: a land region under the control of one government

craftworker: a person who is skilled at a craft, such as a blacksmith, tailor, candlemaker, or cobbler

crisis: a difficult and important time in which the future of things must be determined

cultivate: to help grow

currency: money

customs house: a building where taxes are paid

debate: a discussion where people with different points of view argue their points

deceive: to lie to or betray

deed: a legal paper showing ownership

delegate: someone chosen to speak and act for a group of people

descendant: a person who comes from another person in the same family line

descent: ancestry or family line

diversity: the quality of having people from different cultures or backgrounds

draft: to select people for military service

economy: a way of using resources; the production, use, value, and trade of materials within a state or country

elder: an older person

elevation: how high the land is above sea level

emancipation: freedom, release from slavery

embarkation: getting on a boat to go to sea; starting a journey

empire: a group of countries under one ruler

employee: a person who works for someone else for wages

entice: to tempt or lead on

entrepreneur: a person who has an idea and the courage to start a business

erosion: wearing away of the land by wind or water

evaporate: to turn into vapor and rise

evict: to kick out

excerpt: a small selection taken out of a book, letter, or poem

exclude: to leave out

expense: a cost, money spent in order to make a good or provide a service

express train: a fast train with few stops

famine: a great shortage of food

fatigues: uniforms for soldiers

federal: having to do with the government of the whole country

feminist: having to do with women's rights and equality for women

fertile: allowing lots of things to grow

fiction: something made up

flax: the fiber of a plant used to make cloth

fleet: a group of warships

fossil: the remains of a plant or animal pressed into rock over time

foundry: a building where metal is cast into molds

free enterprise: a system where the people run businesses for profit, and where people buy and sell

freight: a load with goods for transportation, cargo

game: wild animals hunted for food

generation: an entire group of people born and living at the same time

generator: a machine that produces electricity

geography: the study of the earth and the people, animals, and plants living on it

geologist: a scientist who studies the history of the earth through its rocks

glacier: a large mass of ice built up over a long period of time

good: a product that is made, bought, and sold

govern: to rule or control by setting up laws

guarantee: to promise or make sure something happens

habitat: the place or environment in nature where a plant or animal lives

hemp: the fiber of a plant used to make rope and rough cloth

Holocaust: the killing of European Jews in Nazi concentration camps during World War II

human features: things that people build on the land to suit their needs

humid: having a lot of small water droplets in the air

immigrant: a person who moves into a new country to live

immunity: the ability to resist certain diseases

inclined plane: a surface that slopes upward

indentured servant: a person who works for another person for a certain amount of time in order to pay a fee or debt

interpret: to explain the meaning of something

kinsfolk: relatives; family

labor union: a group of workers who get together to cause change

latitude: imaginary lines that measure the distance north or south of the equator

legend: a story passed down through the ages

legislature: the group of people elected to make the laws

liberate: to free

local: close to home

lock: a set of gates used to raise or lower boats as they passed through different water levels

locomotive: an engine used to move railroad cars

longitude: imaginary lines that measure the distance east or west of the prime meridian

loom: a machine that weaves threads of yarn into cloth

Loyalist: a colonist who remained loyal to Great Britain and the king.

luxury: something extra to give pleasure but that is not needed

lye: a harsh substance used in washing and making soap

majority: more than half of the people voting

manufacture: to make something from raw materials

massacre: the violent killing of a number of people

master: the person in charge

mentor: to coach or teach

mercenary: a soldier who is paid to fight in another country

merchant: someone who buys and sells things; a storekeeper

migrant: moving from place to place in order to find work

militiamen: soldiers in the colonial army who could be called on in an emergency

mistreat: to treat badly or abuse

monopoly: when just one company or group owns or controls something

moral: a belief about what is right and what is wrong

natural environment: the surroundings that influence how a plant or animal survives

necessity: something that is needed

origin: beginning

patent: an official paper that says a person invented something

Patriot: a colonist who wanted to break free from Britain's rule

patroon: a person who manages an area of land owned by a country

peninsula: a long narrow piece of land surrounded on three sides with water

permanent: lasting forever or for a long time

persecute: to cause a group to suffer because of their beliefs

plantation: a large farming estate

precipitation: water that falls to the earth as rain, snow, hail, etc.

prejudice: an opinion made of someone before the facts are known; a judgement made about someone because of the color of his or her skin

preservation: guarding or protecting something

profit: the money left after expenses are paid

prohibit: to forbid

proprietors: owners

protest: an organized public demonstration; a complaint against an idea, law, or action

psychology: the study of the human mind and human behavior

quiver: a case for carrying arrows

raceway: a channel dug for water to run through

ramrod: a rod used in loading a cannon or large gun

ratify: to approve

ration: to allow each family only so much food per month in order to make it last as long as possible

raw materials: materials that have not yet been processed or changed, such as logs, minerals, or sheep's wool

rebellion: a fight against those in power

reform: to change in order to make something better

representative: a person elected to vote for other people

reptile: animals that breathe air, have backbones, and are cold-blooded, such as lizards, snakes, alligators, and turtles

research: to study and find out new information about something

reservation: an area of land set aside by the U.S. government for American Indians to live

revolution: a sudden and complete change, such as when one government takes over another, usually by force

riot: a noisy violent uprising

rival: a competitor; someone who tries to equal or outdo someone else

royal: having to do with a king or queen

sacrifice: something you give up in order to have something else

salary: money paid to an employee

sapling: a young tree

sea level: the level of the ocean where it meets the land

segregate: to separate by race

service: something done for another person for money

sinew: a tendon or stringy tissue

slave: a person who is forced to work for someone else without pay

steerage: a section of a ship for passengers paying the lowest fares

stock: a wooden frame with holes for locking in someone's ankles and wrists; money invested in a business

strait: a narrow strip of water connecting two larger bodies of water

strike: a protest where workers stop work until a change or agreement is made

suffrage: the right to vote

sweatshop: a shop or factory where people work for long hours and low wages in unhealthy conditions

symbol: something that stands for something else

tax: money the people give to the government in order to pay for services

tenement: a building, usually run-down, that is divided into apartments for families to rent

tension: a feeling of unrest between people

textile: cloth that is woven or knitted

theory: an idea that has not yet been proven

towpath: a path along a canal from which an animal pulls a boat

toxic: poisonous, very dangerous to your health

tradition: a way of life handed down from parents to children

transistor: a small electronic part that controls the flow of electricity

transmit: to send from one place to another

treason: acting against the government by spying or by threatening to overthrow it

union: a group of workers who get together to cause change

variety: a mix of different things

veto: to reject or say "no" to a bill

voyage: a journey, especially by water from one country to another

wage: money paid to a worker

warping: weaving the threads on a loom to make a woven fabric

woolens: clothes or goods made of wool

INDEX

CREDITS

ART

Burton, Jon 72, 112, 115, 116, 129

Cornia, Ray 22 (lower), 40, 68, 193, 205 (lower), 211, 219

Rasmussen, Gary 10, 18, 21, 22 (upper left), 23, 32, 38 (lower), 41, 42, 53, 71, 81, 83, 97, 132, 133, 161, 213

PHOTOGRAPHS

AP/Wide World Photos 203 (lower)

Barrow, Scott 14 (insert), 15 (lower), 26, 27, 190, 193, 208, 215, 219 (upper), 220 (all), 222

Blanchette, David 33

Chamberlain, Lynn 20 (upper left, lower left)

Choroszewski, Walter 2, 9 (left, lower right), 15 (upper), 18, 104, 126, 166 (lower), 170, 205 (upper), 210, 219 (lower), 221 (all)

Church of Jesus Christ of Latter-Day Saints, The
Historical Department-Archives Division 64 (left)
Museum of History and Art 159 (upper), 169

Colonial Williamsburg 74, 83

CORBIS/Bettmann Archive 177, 187 (left)

DeStafano, Jiacomo 215 (top)

George Eastman House 157, 162, 167

Illinois Historic Preservation Agency 30

Illinois State Historical Society 79 (left), 139 (insert), 146, 153

Johnson&Johnson 217

Kraft, Herbert C., Courtesy of 39, 44 (all)

Kraft, John T. and Susan E. Finn 34, 35, 36 (right), 37, 38 (upper), 43

Lange, Dorothea 182

Library of Congress 66, 79 (upper right)

Lynn, John 19

Michigan Department of State Archives 163

Minnesota Historical Society 36 (left), 134

Museum of the City of New York, The 200 (lower)

NASA 202 (all)

New Jersey Cardinals 203 (upper)

New Jersey Newsphotos 194, 195, 199

New Jersey Office of the Governor 196

North Wind Picture Archives 46, 48, 49, 50, 51, 52, 54, 55, 58, 60, 61, 63, 64 (right), 67, 70, 77 (lower), 78, 82 (lower), 88, 106, 107, 122, 128, 130, 135 (right), 168 (left), 176, 200 (upper), 201 (upper)

Ohio Historical Society 71, 131, 147, 148 (right), 183

PSE&G 218

Rink, Bob 186

Seattle Times 205

Simon, Peter 201 (lower)

Till, Tom 8 (all), 9 (upper right), 11, 13, 14 (background), 17, 24, 124, 127, 154, 174–175 (all)

U.S. Postal Service 184 (upper), 188

Utah State Historical Society 172 (upper), 184 (lower)

Vietnam Memorial, Holmdel 197

Wolfe, Karen M. 204

All photographs not listed are from the collection of Gibbs Smith, Publisher or Anthony DeCondo, author.